Biorhythms

D1603866

BIORHYTHMS

HOW TO LIVE WITH YOUR LIFE CYCLES

BARBARA O'NEIL & RICHARD PHILLIPS

WARD RITCHIE PRESS · PASADENA

To all the people
who we hope will live happier
and more peaceful lives
as a result of this book.

Cover design by Mike Dooley
Illustrations by Jack Matthews

Copyright © 1975 by Barbara O'Neil Phillips and Richard V. Phillips
Library of Congress Catalog Card Number 75-40
ISBN 0378-08199-3 (cloth)
ISBN 0378-08192-6 (paper)
Printed in the United States of America

CONTENTS

PREFACE

We'd like to extend our thanks to those who shared their knowledge and experience with us. You will meet them in the following pages.

We hope this book will give you the opportunity to familiarize yourself with biorhythms and to appreciate the relevance they can have to your own life. Perhaps the book can also contribute, in however small a way, to encouraging an atmosphere in which more serious study of the implications of biorhythm theory—particularly in terms of industrial accident prevention—can take place.

1 THE NATURE OF BIORHYTHMS

Haven't you had days when life seems the proverbial bowl of pitless cherries? When you know for a fact that you can handle anything. But then haven't you found, down the way a bit from such elevations, those other days? The seemingly interminable temporal expanses through which you wander, afflicted by physical, emotional, and intellectual butterfingeritis. These fluctuations are not punishments meted out by a malicious fate operating on the P. T. Barnum theory. Such changes in physical coordination, in mood, in mental acumen, as well as the intervening modulations, occur in cycles, broadly analogous to the more immediately perceptible rhythms of waking and sleeping, inhaling and exhaling.

Through the theory of biorhythm—literally, life's cadence—you can acquaint yourself with and *use*, not be used by, your own tides of vitality.

Pioneers in Biorhythm Study

Those tides were studied extensively, at the turn of the century, by Dr. Wilhelm Fliess in Berlin and by Dr. Hermann Swoboda in Vienna. Fliess, through his observation and documentation of numerous instances of periodic illness, became convinced that certain fundamental rhythms were at work which influenced the onset and disappearance of fevers and respiratory infections. His conclusions about the duration and the significance of such cycles were the same as those reached separately by Swoboda, who also examined many cases of recurrent disease as well as apparently cyclical emotional fluctuations. Empirical discovery and mathematical determination of these patterns of rhythmicity led to the description of a twenty-three-day cycle affecting the physical condition and of a twenty-eight-day cycle influencing the emotional state, or sensitivity. Several years later, in Innsbruck, Dr. Teltscher discerned what seemed to be regular changes in his students' ability to learn. Basing his conclusions on test results and on subsequent observations, he posited a thirty-three-day cycle of mental power.

Biorhythm Theory

Simply, then, the biorhythm theory states that at the moment of birth (the first breath), three cycles which recur consistently throughout one's life are initiated: the physical cycle with a duration of twenty-three days, the sensitivity cycle of twenty-eight days, and the intellectual cycle of thirty-three days. The significant points in each cycle occur at the beginning, or the periodic day, and at the midpoint, or the half-periodic day. These are called critical days—critical in the sense of a turning point—when a cycle changes from the plus or discharge phase (high) to the minus or recharge phase (low), or vice versa.

First of all, the influence of the cycles depends on your age, education, health, circumstances, and, indeed, on your personality. A critical physical day, for example, does not affect everyone in the same way. And second, critical days account for a relatively small percentage of the days in your life. The switch points in any of the cycles should not be cause for alarm, or for giving in to what could be mistaken for a self-fulfilling prophecy. If you know in advance when those times will occur, you can simply be prepared. And, with a little extra care, you can probably make it through the day quite well.

Understanding Yourself Through Biorhythm Theory

But biorhythms are not magic. They will not change your moods or cause them to disappear; they do not mean you'll never make a mistake, never have an accident. Knowledge of your physical, sensitivity, and intellectual cycles *can* get you more in tune with yourself, so you spend less time and effort working at cross-purposes to your energies. And these days, when the times seem perennially out of joint, and when the individual human being seems an endangered species, understanding biorhythms can be especially valuable to you.

What makes your biorhythm chart of singular importance to you is the way you act and react, the kind of personality you are. Awareness is what's paramount. Your chart will show your highs, lows, and critical days; it's up to you to work *with* them, to exercise or to conserve the energies you have.

Say, for example, your day is largely spent fulfilling a child's needs and wants. Do you sometimes feel so harassed that your utmost need is a place to yell or have a good cry? And other days, do you draw on an apparently endless supply of patience, stamina, and smiles? Perhaps you've wondered whether the child had access to the devil's mail or whether you were a minimum of two different people. Or perhaps you experienced the frustrating necessity of affixing blame or accepting guilt, all for what seemed to be inexplicable varieties of mood.

Biorhythms can help you avoid being victimized or totally taken over by those changes by showing you the pattern of their occurrence. And if you're aware of your own personal cadence, you can deal with your low times—compensating where necessary, perhaps practicing self-tolerance—and you can actively use your good times. You'll still experience ups and downs, but biorhythms can show you that you don't have to be at their mercy.

Using Biorhythms

Perhaps your occupation requires manual labor, either in a plant or on a farm, for instance. Have you noticed that some days you can do a tremendous amount of work and not overtax yourself, days when you feel you've really hit your stride? Then, other times, do you find that the day is one big yawn, or do you watch yourself drop almost everything you try to hold, misunderstand instructions, make errors that bring you close to having accidents you don't comprehend? Biorhythms can show you the cyclical nature both of days that seem one long eight-hour proof of ineptitude and of those productive days you feel good about. Such fluctuations are experienced by everyone, though in differing degrees. Biorhythms can alert you to those changes in your physical capacities and abilities, and if you know that a particular day could develop into a real loser, you can try to consider beforehand each of your actions and pace yourself, instead of just having at it.

Or perhaps your work depends on intellectual creativity, be it writing, painting, or corporate decision-making. Have you felt that at times you have the benefit of a perceptive, active and acutely reactive mind, when you consider and formulate a decision quickly and accurately? And then other days your brain seems to give you, at best, flat, discontinuous service? Biorhythms can indicate for you that your ability to concentrate does vary, as does your ability to retain ideas. Being aware of that pattern, you can make the most of your periods of mental vitality and not become disconsolate when that cycle switches into something less than a gangbusters phase.

No matter what your daily round, biorhythms can benefit you. Your biorhythm chart is, in fact, an aid, not a fiat, and with it you can better run your life. A critical day does not equal a stay-in-bed day; that work still has to get done. But knowing what and where your cycles are can help you protect, when necessary, your own natural resources.

Charting Biorhythms

The Physical Cycle

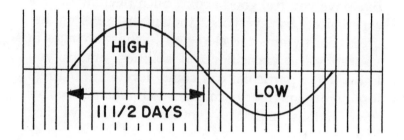

Fig. 1. The physical rhythm

Each rhythm can be graphically represented. In the course of the twenty-three-day physical cycle, the first eleven and a half days are known as the plus or discharge period. This is a time of increased vitality, of good coordination, of physical competence and stamina. During the second part of the cycle, the minus or recuperative phase, there is a lessening of energy (you may tire more easily) and a need for rest. On the critical days, the beginning and the midpoint of the physical cycle, the body is in a state of flux, neither plus nor minus, if you will. This "up-for-grabs" period, believed to last for twenty-four hours, means that there is an increased potential for error and for accident.

This potential is most certainly *not* an absolute guarantee of disaster. Far from it. What the critical days in the physical cycle indicate is a possibility of physical ineptitude, mainly because at those times your body is in a transition period. Your physical ability is, at the very least, in question. It would seem wise, then, to be more careful, more aware of what you're doing, on critical physical days.

The Sensitivity Cycle

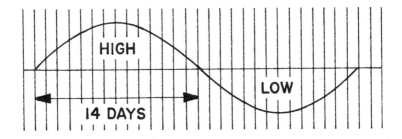

Fig. 2. The sensitivity rhythm

In the twenty-eight-day sensitivity cycle, the first fourteen days are the plus period, when feelings of cheerfulness and general goodwill prevail. During the second part of this rhythm, there's a sense of emotional negativism, even flatness, and edginess. The critical days, at the beginning and at the midpoint of this cycle, when the nervous system is switching from discharge to recharge (or vice versa), also indicate a potential for accident. The sensitivity cycle seems to influence not only your emotional outlook but your reactive ability as well. So, depending on your circumstances and your personality, you could be more irritable, say, and therefore less able to cope because everyone and everything get to you. You're more apt to make mistakes

7

because you haven't the patience to do your work with your usual care and thoroughness. Again, if you know when your critical sensitivity days occur, you can make allowances for your mood and attitude.

The Intellectual Cycle

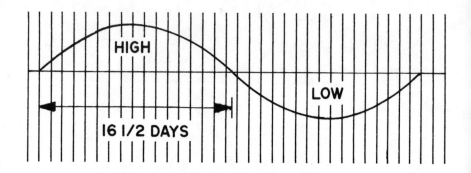

Fig. 3. The intellectual rhythm

During the first sixteen and a half days of the intellectual cycle, the plus or discharge period, your mental powers are most active—you can learn new material more readily, your memory functions better, you can think more clearly. The second sixteen-and-a-half-day span seems more conducive to consolidating what you've learned. In this cycle, the critical days, the beginning and the midpoint, indicate a reduced ability to concentrate and to think things through. If a decision has to be made on a critical intellectual day, you should perhaps take a little extra time to be sure you've adequately considered all aspects of the problem. If those days of transition are recognized for the influence they could have, you can surmount what may seem to be your hibernating brain.

Interpreting Your Cycles

Talking about each rhythm separately is misleading in a way, for all three operate in concert. They do not occur individually. Together, they affect people differently. In the interpretation of your biorhythm chart, do not be put off by the appearance of approximately six critical days every month. That does not mean that you will necessarily have six rotten days per month. Biorhythms do not *determine* how you will act and feel; rather, they indicate potentials.

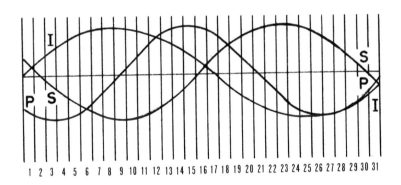

Fig. 4. A complete biorhythm chart

Examine, for instance, the above chart. The critical physical days occur on the ninth and the twenty-first of this particular month. In the first case, the intellectual cycle is at a high point while the sensitivity cycle is at a low. Here, a temperamental individual upset at witnessing his physical ineptness might, therefore, make more errors than usual, because he wants to get home as fast as possible so the day will end. For an individual of more even disposition, this day might be marked by just feeling a bit blue, rather out of sorts. He might feel sharp enough mentally, but not really interested in exercising that capacity. If someone is more physically oriented, however, this day could be one to be ready for. He should probably pay more attention when he drives, because his reaction time could be impaired. At his job, he would be wise to watch himself, especially if his work is hazardous. There is a potential here for error, perhaps for accident, which should be taken into account.

The critical sensitivity days occur here on the second, the sixteenth, and the thirtieth. On the sixteenth, for example, the physical rhythm is at a high, while the intellectual rhythm is approaching a critical day. For an excitable person, this day could become a series of overextensions. The physical high, with its energy and sense of exuberant muscle-flexing, could tax the nervous system to the extent that the individual might feel tired and irritated because he tried to cope with too many things. Someone with a more even temperament might have a fairly good day, with the physical cycle compensating for the critical sensitivity day. But, too, external circumstances could be such that the critical day would leave him feeling harassed by too many people with one too many irrelevant things to say. For a person who could be described as physical, the sixteenth might be a fine day with everything going smoothly. Or the physical high might not offset the critical sensitivity day, and he might find himself, in an excess of feeling good, taking on riskier tasks, perhaps creating a situation where an accident might occur.

In Figure 4, the critical intellectual days occur on the first, and on the seventeenth, with the physical rhythm having passed its peak and the sensitivity cycle on the upswing. This day might be characterized by a rather frustrating inability to make a decision, though the positions of the other two rhythms could be compensatory. A highly strung person might find himself snapping at everyone, while a calmer individual might react a bit more than usual to minor annoyances. Perhaps for someone physically oriented, the seventeenth would be a really good day, with the critical intellectual state passing unnoticed.

Each of the cycles has its own general attributes; they are all interrelated. But each individual acts and reacts differently. Where a critical sensitivity day might drive one person up the wall, the same day might, in someone else, give no external indications of its existence. As noted above, critical days form a relatively small percentage of one's life. But, as we'll see later, they can be significant in cases of self-caused accidents, and it is prudent to consider such days so you can be alert to their effects on you.

Relationships with Others

Biorhythm can also offer insights into your relationships with others. The observation that someone is having a bad day may have sound basis in his biorhythmic state. The person in question may be experiencing a critical day or a full low in at least two rhythms. Knowing about life cycles in yourself and in others won't change the fact that such ups and downs exist. But if the usually genial person where you work is grouchy and doesn't tell even one of his awful jokes, instead of dismissing his mood with exasperation, a biorhythmically informed you might be a bit more empathic. Or perhaps there is a person you are unable to work closely with. The reason might be that your respective cycles offer few points of compatibility.

In these kinds of personal observations biorhythm theory can be helpful to you. It does not pretend to control the externals in your life: it offers a way of helping deal with yourself, a way of coping. Your cyclical fluctuations are not peculiarly your own. Two people born on the same day would have the same biorhythm charts. But for a person born early in the morning, the critical days would occur almost a full day earlier than those of another person born near midnight of the same day. What effectively personalizes your biorhythm chart is your awareness of the way you act and feel at certain points in the cycles.

Computing Your Own Biorhythms

Computing your biorhythms involves dividing the number of days you have lived by the number of days in each rhythm. If you are something less than mathematically inclined, or if numbers make you uncomfortable, you can send your birth date, and a fee, to Human Bio Rhythms Corporation, a California firm specializing in providing biorhythm charts

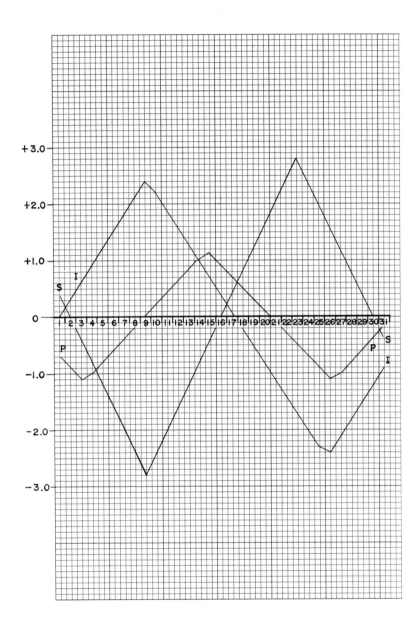

Fig. 5. Another form for a complete biorhythm chart

and interpretations. (See page 104 for details). You can, of course, do your own chart following the method outlined in Chapter Five.

Once you determine the position of your cycles, you can prepare a chart in the form shown in Figure 4. Or the same information can be represented in a graph, as in Figure 5. Both are regulation biorhythm charts. You can use either one.

A new computation has been developed by Richard Phillips especially for this book: the composite, which is derived from the points used in plotting the graph. Figure 6 shows the composite graph for Figure 5. (The actual process of determining the composite for any chart is explained in detail in Chapter Six.)

Briefly, the composite represents the algebraic sum of values assigned to each day of each cycle. This

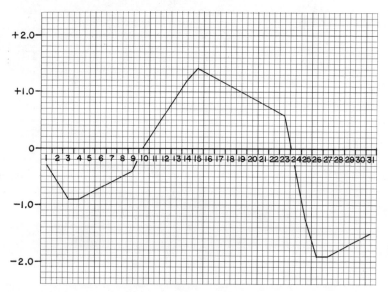

Fig. 6. The composite

single line takes into account general personality traits, and it can, therefore, be more directly relevant to you. It is especially valuable in compatibility studies and for a general overview of your own chart.

All in all, learning about biorhythms can make just plain coping a bit easier. Awareness of these three cycles in your life can perhaps save you some of the worry that may accompany the less-than-good times, and can help you take full advantage of your good times.

2 NOTABLES AND LIFE CYCLES

Plus . . . critical day . . . minus . . . critical day . . .
What does the times-three togetherness in a biorhythm chart mean? As you might expect, there is
no basic formula for interpretation that always
applies. You can't, for example, look at a chart, even
for a known hara-kiri victim, and say, "Elementary,
Watson, 'tis a classic case of suicide." A biorhythm
chart is one way of expressing an individual's
condition. If you superimpose on that pattern the
fact of an event, the result is a graphic perspective in
which to consider that person during a given period
of time. You can quite literally see the movement of
the life cycles—the fluctuations in physical, emotional, and intellectual energies—which surround the
event, the whole patterns in which those single days
occur.

William McKinley

Examine, for instance, the biorhythm chart for
William McKinley; it encompasses the time from

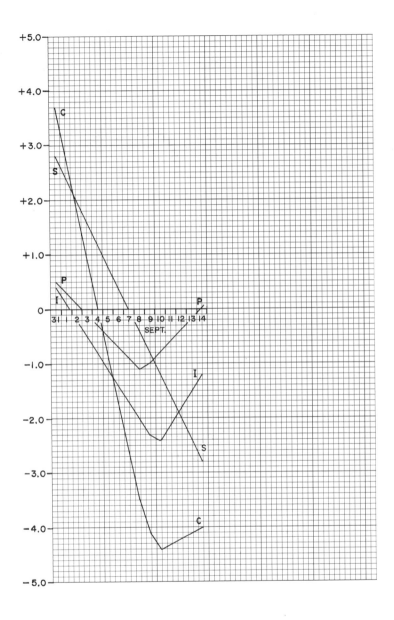

Fig. 7. William McKinley (b. Jan 29, 1843)
Aug. 31 - Sept. 14, 1901

August 31 to the president's death on September 14, 1901. After a critical day on the first, the intellectual rhythm moves into the minus phase, down to a full low on the tenth and starts upward again. The sensitivity cycle descends from a peak on August 31 to a nadir on the fourteenth. The physical rhythm switches into low on the third and reaches another critical day on the fourteenth. The general, even cumulative, effect of those alterations is represented in the steep decline of the composite.

McKinley was attending the Pan-American Exposition in Buffalo, New York, when he was shot once by an assassin on September 6, 1901. The chart says nothing about that particular event. McKinley was not predisposed biorhythmically to having an attempt made on his life. The chart does suggest, in the combination of a low in sensitivity and a critical physical day, reduced strength and perhaps a lessened resistance. The slight upturn in the composite reflects the movement toward the plus phase of the physical and intellectual cycles, but the change is so gradual that already depleted reserves might not be able to respond to stress adequately.

Newspaper reports at the time had McKinley steadily recovering until September 13, when he suffered a relapse. His death coincided with a critical physical day. Though the low in all three rhythms, and their effective influence demonstrated in the composite, appear hardly conducive to recovery, we cannot say that McKinley's chart *explains* his death. Rather, the particular biorhythmic configuration is one set of circumstances in which the death occurred. It is one way of looking at that event. Perhaps in cases of serious illness or injury, a critical physical day is a kind of crisis point which must be overcome before real healing can begin. And if one is further weakened by lows in the sensitivity and intellectual cycles, the energy needed to withstand the strain may not be there in sufficient quantity.

Harry Houdini

An analogous situation is represented in the chart for Harry Houdini, whose name has become synonymous with great escapes—especially from locked, roped, and weighted containers while he was handcuffed and otherwise shackled. During the course of the two-week period, all three rhythms switch into minus phases and the composite descends sharply, leveling off on the twenty-ninth. And what happened while the life cycles were changing in that way?

On October 19, after a lecture in Montreal, Houdini's comments about the strength of his stomach muscles provoked a student to strike him twice in the abdomen. Later, in Detroit, Houdini underwent surgery for the consequent appendicitis and developed peritonitis. A second operation, on October 29, for that condition was not successful. Houdini died on October 31, 1926. His chart shows an absolute low in the physical rhythm on the twenty-ninth. That, combined with lows in the other two rhythms, may have further reduced Houdini's ability to tolerate shock to his system. The picture here is of recuperative powers sorely tested, with no cycles in plus phases.

If in these two charts there's a story to be told, the composites seem to be the narrators. At times when McKinley and Houdini could surely have benefited

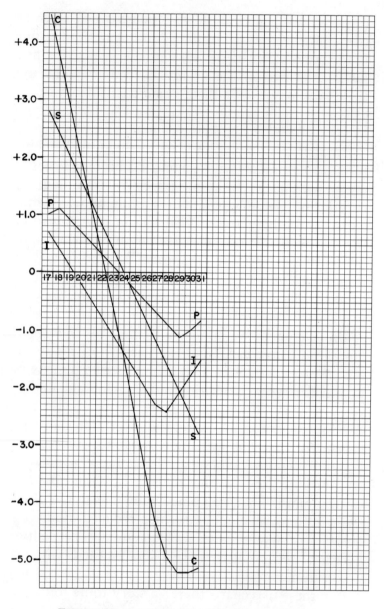

Fig. 8. Harry Houdini (b. Apr. 6, 1874)
Oct. 17 - 31, 1926

from strength and energy to be expended, those single lines show a further draining of already depleted reserves. The composites offer a significant view of changes in energy levels. Although those alterations do not *cause* good or poor health, they do suggest that the body's ability to deal with trauma is greater at certain times than at others. And if a biorhythmic pattern of lows in the cycles is the context in which injury or illness occurs, the process of recovery may prove too much of a strain, as the charts for McKinley and Houdini demonstrate.

Judy Garland

Judy Garland: her very name evokes memories of the wondrous charm of Dorothy in her red spangled shoes going off to see the Wizard, and of the painful unevenness of the real woman's career. She was found dead in her London home on June 22, 1969, a victim of accidental barbiturate poisoning. In Judy Garland's chart for the days preceding her death, all three rhythms move from plus to minus phases: a critical intellectual day on the eighteenth followed on the twentieth by a critical sensitivity day, with the physical cycle approaching a critical day. The composite shows the steady downward trend of her energies after the thirteenth. Those mental and emotional changes could have underscored feelings of upset, depression, or lack of control. Further, the crossing of the intellectual and sensitivity and then of the physical and sensitivity rhythms could have made a sense of personal crisis and futility acute. And the significance of certain actions might have been obscured by depth of feeling. These particular

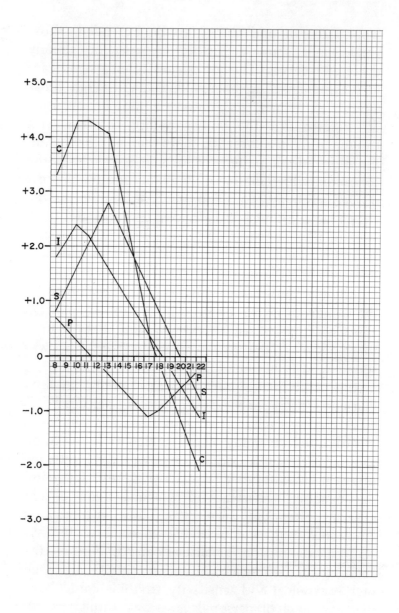

Fig. 9. Judy Garland (b. June 10, 1922)
June 8 - 22, 1969

cyclical influences shown in Judy Garland's bio-rhythm chart offer one perspective on the disposition of her natural powers, one that becomes tragic in its abrupt end.

Janis Joplin

Figure 10 is a biorhythm chart for Janis Joplin, as renowned for her Southern Comfort and outrageous costumes as for her flamboyantly unorthodox style of singing. In Myra Friedman's biography, *Buried Alive*, Janis Joplin comes across as an agonizingly troubled woman whose career, after several lulls and fresh starts, was beginning to reflect her own development as an artist. She died of an accidental overdose of heroin on October 4, 1970. Her chart depicts the physical cycle on the upswing after a critical day on the third, and the sensitivity rhythm still in the plus phase, though approaching a critical day. The intellectual cycle is in a low phase. The overall direction of those changes is shown in the composite, which enters the minus phase on October 1.

Friends were vaguely uneasy about her state on the third, but there was no overt indication of great personal upset. Janis Joplin's chart shows a particular set of internal circumstances that accompanied her death at the age of twenty-seven.

Marilyn Monroe

The biorhythm chart for the days preceding Marilyn Monroe's death is found in Figure 11. The woman whose name conjured images of unrelieved sexuality was found dead in her Hollywood home on August 5, 1962, an empty pill bottle at her side. In her chart, the intellectual rhythm is descending but

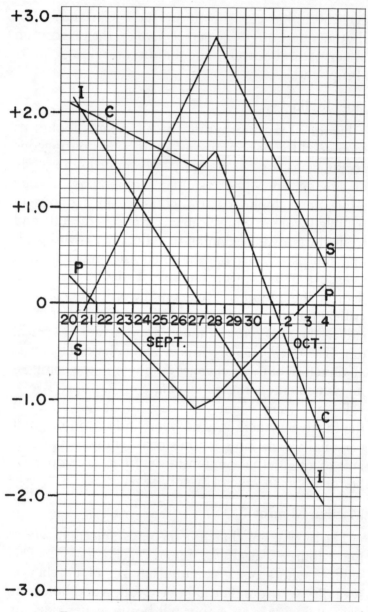

Fig. 10. Janis Joplin (b. Jan. 19, 1943)
Sept. 20 - Oct. 4, 1970

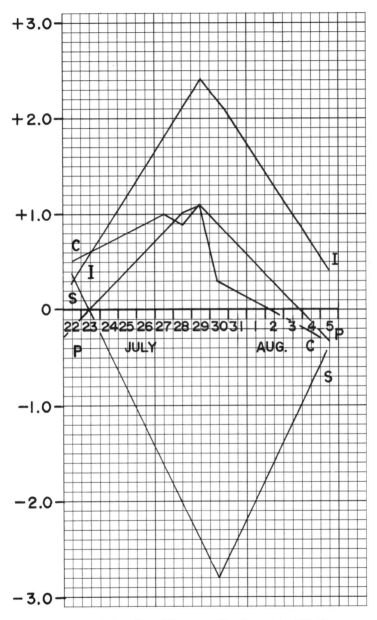

Fig. 11. Marilyn Monroe (b. June 1, 1926)
July 22 - Aug. 5, 1962

still in the plus phase, the sensitivity cycle is approaching the median line, and the physical rhythm switches into low on August 3. The composite, after July 29, drops sharply, entering the minus phase on August 20. The position of the physical and intellectual cycles, combined with the sensitivity rhythm still in low, could have made unhappiness seem dominant.

In the charts for Judy Garland, Janis Joplin, and Marilyn Monroe, the physical and sensitivity rhythms are almost mirror images, with the peak in one nearly directly above the absolute low in the other. In addition, the composite in all three cases crossed the median line into a low phase a few days before the death occurred. The intellectual cycle for Marilyn Monroe is the only one to be in the plus period. The general comparison of these charts does reveal similarities, but no one biorhythmic picture of a potential suicide emerges. The charts show the cycles of internal influences; the coinciding events point to the ways different personalities modulate and deal with those influences.

James Dean

On September 30, 1955, James Dean was killed in a head-on collision just outside of Paso Robles, California. The actor, who seemed almost a spokesman for a generation because of his role in *Rebel Without a Cause*, had completed the film *Giant* and was going to Salinas in his new Porsche for the races. His biorhythm chart (Fig. 12) shows the physical rhythm in the plus phase, as is the sensitivity cycle (though approaching a critical day), while

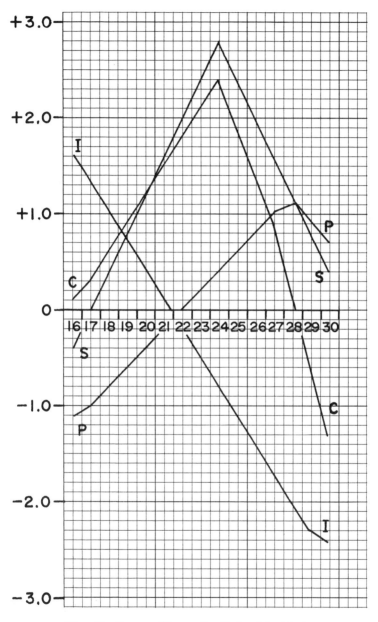

Fig. 12. James Dean (b. Feb. 8, 1931)
Sept. 16 - 30, 1955

the intellectual rhythm is in a full low. The composite, after reaching a peak on the twenty-fourth, drops sharply toward the switch point on the twenty-eighth. That biorhythmic situation suggests a lessened ability to think clearly and decide quickly, as well as relatively slower reflexes. And perhaps there was a certain amount of physical tiredness and a preoccupation with what would happen in Salinas, all of which contributed to a tragic accident—and the popular canonization of James Dean.

Duke Ellington

Duke Ellington, world-famous musician and goodwill ambassador, entered a New York hospital at the end of March, 1974, for treatment of lung cancer. His condition worsened and he developed pneumonia. He died on May 24, 1974. Duke Ellington's chart (Fig. 13) shows the changes in the biorhythm cycles in the two-week period before his death. The intellectual rhythm is in low; the sensitivity cycle is approaching a peak; the physical rhythm is descending toward a critical day. The composite moves from a low, through the switch point on the twenty-third, into the plus phase. Perhaps this crossing was as significant as a critical day: the composite does show the general direction of all energies, and a severely weakened condition might have been unable to tolerate the increased strain of that transition.

Aristotle Onassis

The biorhythm chart for Aristotle Onassis (Figure 14) shows the physical cycle switching into low on the third; the sensitivity rhythm descending to a full

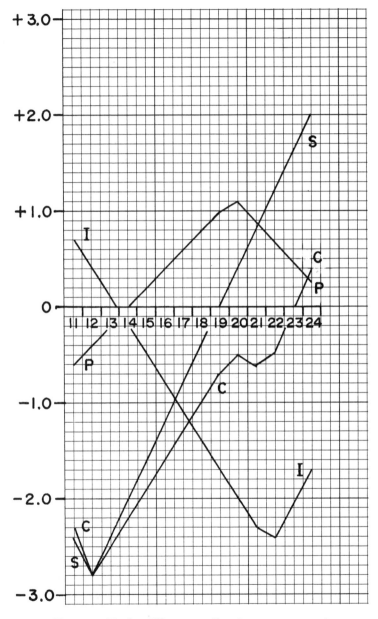

Fig. 13. Duke Ellington (b. Apr. 29, 1899)
May 11 - 24, 1974

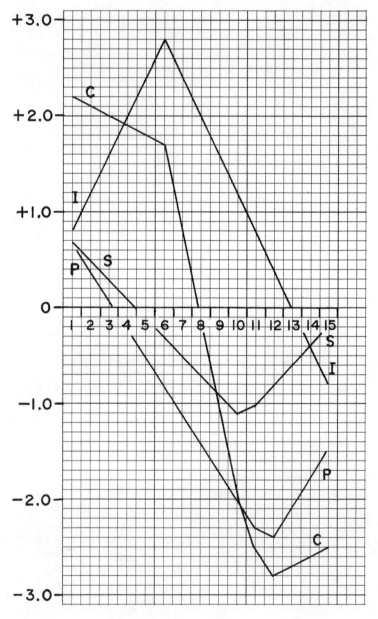

Fig. 14. Aristotle Onassis (b. Jan. 15, 1900)
Mar. 1 - 15, 1975

low and approaching a critical day; and the intellectual cycle moving into the minus phase on the thirteenth. The composite goes into a steep decline on the seventh and begins a slight upward movement after the twelfth.

Onassis, as famous for his millions as for his marriage to Jacqueline Kennedy, entered the American Hospital near Paris in February. He was suffering from myasthenia gravis, a progressive weakening of the voluntary muscles; he underwent surgery shortly thereafter. Onassis' death, on March 15, 1975, was attributed to bronchial pneumonia. In his chart, all rhythms are in low, indicating a lessened capacity for resistance. The crossing of the sensitivity and intellectual rhythms on the fourteenth perhaps had the effect of a critical day, particularly in terms of weakening an already strained system.

Ann-Margret

The next chart shows an entirely different situation. On September 11, 1972, Ann-Margret was to open at the Sahara Tahoe Hotel. Her entrance was to be pure extravaganza: she was to be lowered on a platform down about twenty feet to the stage. What actually happened proved to be a rare test of her courage and determination. Ann-Margret was on that platform just before her act was to begin. Another section of the contraption broke, causing the part on which she was standing to tilt. Her fall resulted in five facial fractures and a broken arm— and months of painful recuperation after the cosmetic surgery which followed.

Ann-Margret's biorhythm chart includes the time of the accident, which occurred on September 11. At that time, the intellectual and sensitivity cycles had

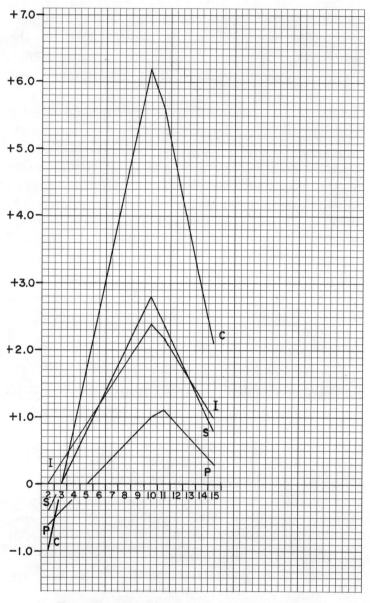

Fig. 15. Ann-Margret (b. Apr. 28, 1941)
Sept. 2 - 15, 1972

just passed their high points and the physical rhythm was at a peak. The influence of all three cycles in the plus phase is shown in the composite, which had, on the eleventh, begun a slight descent from its very high level. On one hand, this biorhythmic position seems especially conducive to successfully beginning new endeavors: the energies were all positive and were there to be drawn upon. On the other, however, this configuration can be seen as advising the individual concerned that even though everything seems so *great,* perhaps a bit of care should be exercised so one does not overextend oneself or throw oneself into a situation where an accident might occur. Certainly, Ann-Margret's chart does not indicate that part of the platform would collapse. Perhaps, however, it would have been wise to avoid a potentially hazardous situation.

Richard Nixon

Figure 16 is a biorhythm chart for Richard Nixon. The period covered includes the day of his resignation, August 9, 1974. On that day, the intellectual rhythm was in low; the sensitivity cycle was just past its peak; the physical rhythm was approaching a critical day. The crossing of the intellectual and physical cycles on the seventh might have accentuated negative feelings and mental and physical exhaustion. The composite shows a general decline in energies after August 8. And certainly the period immediately following the resignation was a time of poor health for Nixon. This chart shows the operation of biorhythmic influences in his life during that time.

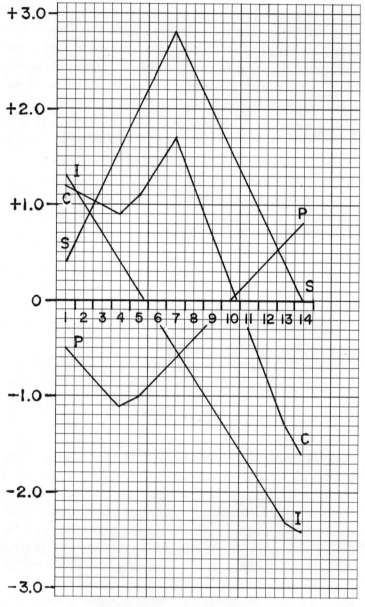

Fig. 16. Richard Nixon (b. Jan. 13, 1913)
Aug. 1 - 14, 1974

Ford's Pardon

It has been said that because President Ford was, biorhythmically, experiencing a physical high and intellectual and sensitivity lows on September 8, 1974, he granted the pardon to Nixon. That statement assumes that Ford considered the information, reached a decision, and acted upon that decision—all in one day. Biorhythm theory is not that presumptuous. It is not an explanation of the present or a prediction of future events.

A biorhythm chart will show you the changing patterns of an individual's vitality, in terms of highs, lows, and critical days. And the charts included in this chapter demonstrate a variety of biorhythmic situations. Not one is an absolute guarantee of success or of failure, or of a fatal mishap or illness. Each chart is an illustration of cyclical influences in an individual's life, a background for certain occurrences. And the more biorhythm charts you see and interpret, the more perceptive you'll become about the workings of the cycles in your own life. Even though another person may have had an entirely different experience, you can become increasingly aware of the way you respond in a particular set of biorhythmic circumstances.

3 BIORHYTHMS IN SPORTS

A biorhythm chart offers one way of looking at an individual in the context of a coincidental event. The influence of the cycles varies, as we saw in the last chapter, and it is possible and desirable to see the biorhythmic process as a challenge, as a set of factors that can be dealt with.

Athletes' concentration on training and conditioning, and on finding and maintaining the game face—that intangible quality of being properly psyched—tends to make them as a group less susceptible to the extremes of biorhythmic influence. But they do have their ups and downs: days when a training program seems impossibly taxing; other times when the same regimen seems a breeze. And we have all seen contests of one sort or another in which some individuals seemed to have come all too recently from the deep freeze. But the relationship between an athlete's performance and his or her biorhythm chart is often a model for coping.

Jesse Owens

Look at Jesse Owens' chart (Figure 17), which covers the time of his remarkable performance in the 1936 Berlin Olympics. On August third, a critical physical day, Owens broke the world record in the quarter-finals and in the finals of the 100-meter dash, though his time was disallowed because of a favoring wind. On the fourth, when the physical and sensitivity cycles were low, he set an Olympic record in the broad jump and shattered all records in the trials for the 200-meter dash, an event he won the next day. And on August eighth, a critical intellectual day, with the other two rhythms in low, Owens was on the winning 400-meter relay team.

The composite is in sharp decline, and the crossing on the third supersedes the critical physical day, effectively raising the biorhythmic odds against extraordinary performance. And Owens had also to contend with official harassment in a variety of guises. Yet he won. The chart offers another view of how amazing Jesse Owens' performance was.

Johnny Miller

Figure 18 is the biorhythm chart for Johnny Miller, during the 1973 U. S. Open Golf Tournament in Oakmont, Pennsylvania. His score for the round on Saturday the sixteenth was a depressing five over par. Going into the final round on June seventeenth, he was six strokes behind the leaders. On that day,

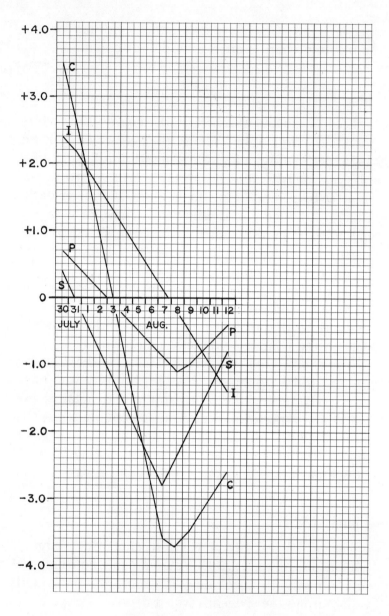

Fig. 17. Jesse Owens (b. Sept. 12, 1913)
July 30 - Aug. 12, 1936

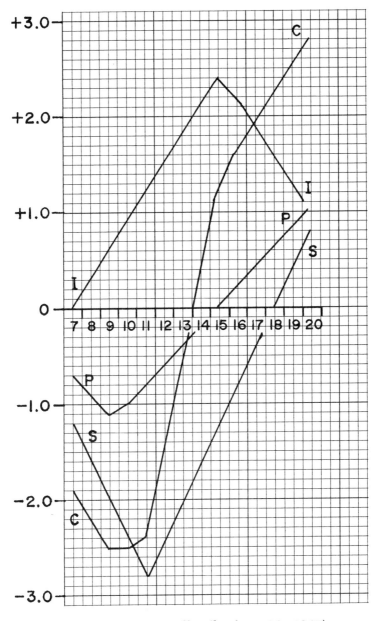

Fig. 18. Johnny Miller (b. Apr. 29, 1947)
June 7 - 20, 1973

the intellectual rhythm was in the plus phase, the physical cycle was on the upswing after a critical day on the fifteenth, and the sensitivity rhythm was approaching a critical day. The composite, a general representation of the combination of the cycles, continued its rise.

On the seventeenth, despite the rain and the heat, Johnny Miller fired a record-breaking 63 and became the U. S. Open champion by one stroke. If we were going strictly by his chart, the nineteenth or twentieth would have been a better time for him to have played the final round. But in terms of the composite, which was moving strongly upward on the seventeenth, Johnny Miller's level of competitive performance was high.

Kareem Abdul-Jabbar

In the biorhythm chart for Kareem Abdul-Jabbar, the sensitivity rhythm moves toward a critical day on October eighth, the physical cycle reaches a peak on the fourth, and the intellectual rhythm switches into the plus phase on the second. The composite shows a rise, leveling off on the fifth.

Jabbar is not renowned for his calmness of temper on the court, but Saturday, October 5, 1974, when the Milwaukee Bucks played the Boston Celtics, marked a rare display. Jabbar was poked in the left eye by Don Nelson of the Celtics during that preseason game. Jabbar was so angry, he punched a basket support and broke his hand. Perhaps the crossing of the intellectual and physical cycles on the fifth helped create a certain internal tension which, on that occasion, was provoked into a physical release.

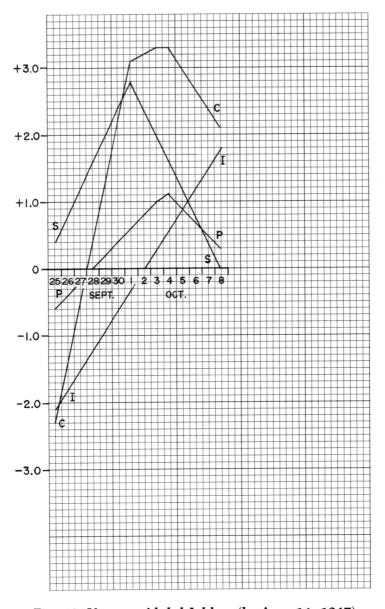

Fig. 19. Kareem Abdul-Jabbar (b. Apr. 16, 1947)
Sept. 25 - Oct. 8, 1974

Billie Jean King

Billie Jean King's chart, for the time of the match in Houston on September 20, 1973, shows the sensitivity and intellectual rhythms approaching their peak while the physical rhythm has just passed its lowest point. The composite illustrates the strength of the positive phase. And she beat Bobby Riggs, who was, according to some reports, biorhythmically low. His chart isn't included here because it's difficult to find a consistent birth date for him.

Though it was hardly the victory or the defeat that all the feminist/chauvinist puffery surrounding the match would have it to be, Billie Jean King happened to play when most of her energies were there to be used. Certainly her training and conditioning, and her being obviously up for playing Riggs, helped compensate for the physical low.

Wilt Chamberlain

On March 2, 1962, a basketball player scored 100 points—in one game. Wilt Chamberlain, playing for the Philadelphia Warriors then, hit 36 of 63 field goals and 28 of 32 free throws, both record numbers of attempts for him. His biorhythm chart does not suggest that March 2 would be a great day. The intellectual cycle was at a switch point; the physical rhythm was still in the plus phase, having passed its peak; and the sensitivity rhythm was approaching a critical day and actually crossed the intellectual cycle on the second—a potentially disconcerting configuration. Further, the composite shows a tapering off toward the minus phase, switching on the third.

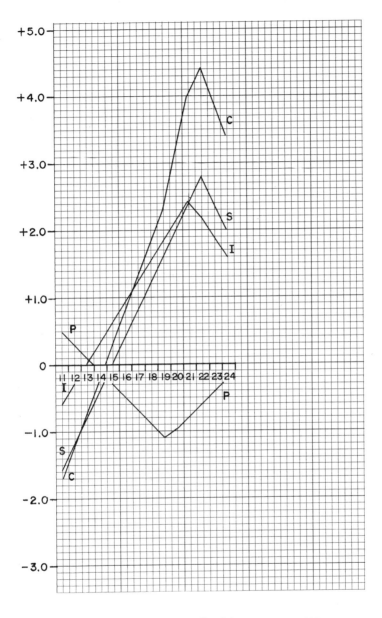

Fig. 20. Billie Jean King (b. Nov. 22, 1943)
Sept. 11 - 24, 1973

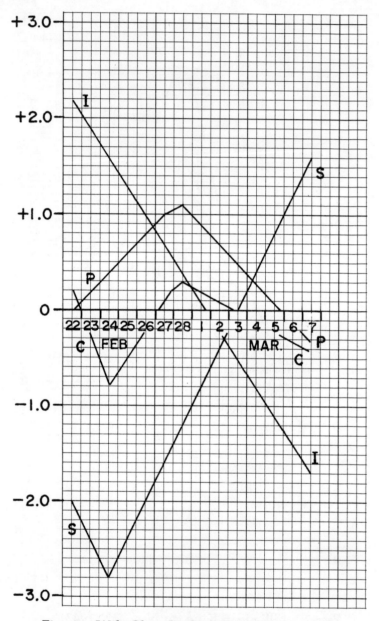

Fig. 21. Wilt Chamberlain (b. Aug. 21, 1936)
Feb. 22 - Mar. 7, 1962

Chamberlain admits in his autobiography that his teammates, aware of his chance to score 100 points, fed him the ball even when they had clear shots. But had he not been hitting, he would not have been able to set a record that still stands.

Olga Korbut

The chart for Olga Korbut, the young Russian gymnast, appears in Figure 22. The time period includes her performance during the 1972 Olympics in Munich. The progressive downward trend of her energies is graphically demonstrated in the composite, which goes into a steep decline after August twenty-fourth.

Olga Korbut was the first person to do a backward somersault on the uneven parallel bars in competition—and she charmed almost everyone. She had been performing beautifully and was leading the Russian team, when, on August 30, she fell to the floor from the uneven parallel bars. As stunned and dismayed as her audience, she finished her routine, and the next day was awarded a silver medal in individual competition for her performance.

On the basis of her chart, the thirtieth was not an especially promising day: physical and sensitivity cycles in low, the intellectual rhythm still in the plus phase but descending toward the switch point. And the composite crossed into low the previous day. Perhaps the break in concentration and her fall, as well as the pressure of being in the Olympics, combined with the cyclic influences shown here, persuaded Olga Korbut that the rest she took after the games ended was necessary.

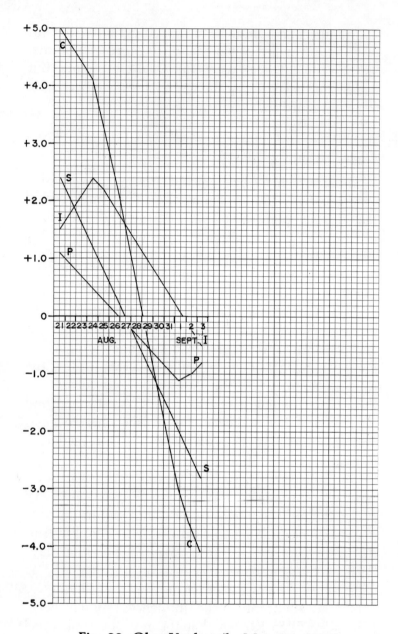

Fig. 22. Olga Korbut (b. May 16, 1955)
Aug. 21 - Sept. 3, 1972

Muhammad Ali and George Foreman

The following charts (Figures 23 and 24) are for Muhammad Ali and George Foreman at the time of the title bout in Kinshasa, Zaire. Ali's chart shows, on October 29, 1974, a critical physical day and the sensitivity and intellectual rhythms in low. Foreman's chart, on the other hand, reveals all three cycles in the plus phase. And Foreman was the 3-to-1 favorite. But Ali won by a knockout in the eighth round.

A compatibility chart for the two boxers, whose verbal sparring gained as much attention as the actual fight, is shown in Figure 25. Only the composites are included here, yet it is clear that, strictly in terms of the chart, Foreman as favorite was not an unreasonable choice—and between the boxers themselves, there appears minimal chance for a mutual admiration society.

The charts included here offer a wide range of biorhythmic situations. A comparison of the charts for Jesse Owens, Olga Korbut, and Muhammad Ali indicates that critical days and lows do not guarantee mistakes or failure; the charts for Johnny Miller, Billie Jean King, and George Foreman show that highs do not necessarily mean success. We must keep in mind that in all these equations, training is crucial, and a certain amount of circumspection in interpretation is needed to allow for its effects.

A consideration of the charts here and in the previous chapter, in connection with certain events, points to the variety of biorhythmic situations and their influences. In that context, biorhythm can be seen as a contributory factor—as, for example, in the case of Olga Korbut—and you can develop a

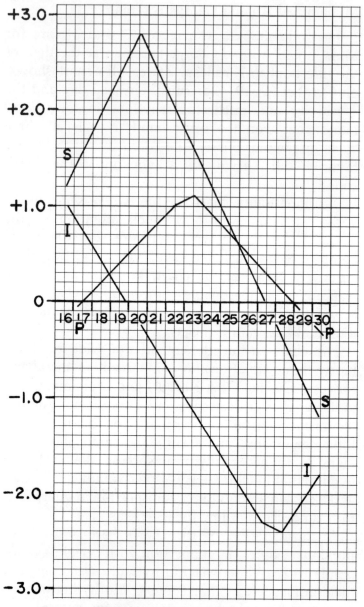

Fig. 23. Muhammad Ali (b. Jan. 17, 1942)
Oct. 16 - 30, 1974

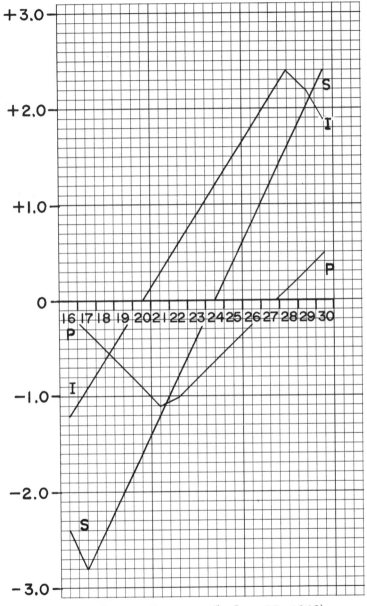

Fig. 24. George Foreman (b. Jan. 22, 1948)
Oct. 16 - 30, 1974

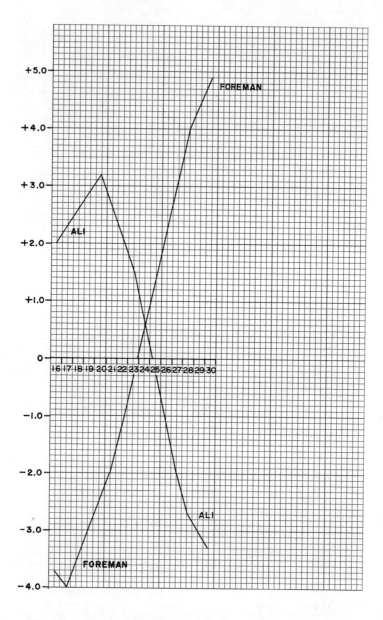

Fig. 25. Compatibility chart for Ali and Foreman

perspective on its workings, a view that encompasses the information contained in the chart itself as well as the general personality and circumstances of the individual in question. You don't have to see biorhythm as predestination. There are cycles in all our lives to which we respond and react differently, but what's important is that you gain a sense of the nuances of biorhythm so you can approach its influence in your life realistically.

4 BIORHYTHMIC CYCLES AND INDUSTRIAL ACCIDENT PREVENTION

It's easy enough to agree with the observation that people have good days and bad days, that human performance varies. Indeed, all industrial safety programs implicitly recognize that fact. And it's also easy enough to agree with the goal of any such program: a zero accident rate. Employers and employees alike look forward to achieving this ideal work state. The difficulty, as you might suspect and as usual, lies between the real and the utopian. What sort of safety program will effectively minimize the number of accidents? Machinery will malfunction and acts of God will occur, but how do you deal with human error, the causative factor in most mishaps?

Posters alone are ineffective. Repeated lectures eventually fall on eat-your-spinach-deafened ears. Such methods are, in a sense, an externalized approach to the question of safety. They are an attempt to impose a constant on individuals, a level of consistently errorless performance. This is not to suggest that the goal of an ever-lower accident rate should be abandoned as unrealistic. Not at all. But perhaps an approach from the inside, as it were, one that not only assumes but tries to work *through* or *with* human variability, could make an existing industrial safety program more effective.

Biorhythms and Accidents

One way of getting at the "inside," the fluctuations in individual performance, is offered by biorhythms. According to the theory, such changes recur in specific cycles, and at the switch points in the physical, sensitivity, and intellectual rhythms, there is an increased potential for mishap. What sort of relationship exists between critical days and accidents? Several studies have examined precisely that question.

Recent Studies

Russell K. Anderson, retired president of R. K. Anderson Associates, Inc., safety consultants, has reported on the firm's extensive research into biorhythms. In the early sixties, a three-year study involved a knitting mill, and metal-working, textile, and chemical plants. More than three hundred accidents, each one detailed in workmen's compensation records, were analyzed in terms of the individual and his biorhythmic cycles. Anderson found that almost seventy percent of those industrial accidents occurred on a critical day for the person involved. Subsequent investigations, covering the years 1970 through 1972, conducted in the same four industries and in a die-casting company, revealed that of approximately one thousand accidents, analyzed as in the earlier study, ninety percent took place on a critical day for the individual involved.

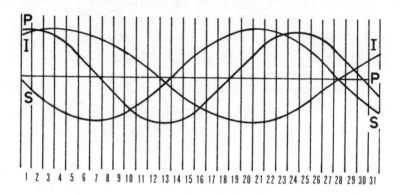

Fig. 26. One biorhythm configuration indicating potential for accident

In the above hypothetical chart, the physical cycle is at its lowest point, the intellectual and sensitivity cycles cross just below the median line (on the thirteenth). Anderson has found that this situation can have the effect of a triple-critical day, when all cycles reach a switch point at the same time. His analyses indicated that some of the more serious accidents occurred when the individual was in just this biorhythmic position and, further, that the closer to the median line the crossing, the more serious the accident appeared to be.

On a more informal level, Major Tim Brady examined fifty-nine accidents, attributed either to pilot error or to undetermined causes, that had occurred within the Tactical Air Command over a three-year period. There had been four other crashes, but birth dates for the pilots in question were unavailable. Of the total, thirteen coincided with a critical day for at least one of the pilots involved. Major Brady also notes, in the March 1972 issue of *TAC Attack*, that in forty of the fifty-nine accidents (or sixty-seven percent), two or three biorhythm cycles for at least one pilot were in low or minus phases.

Cyrus B. Newcomb, Jr., in his October 1974 address to the Edison Electric Institute Accident Prevention Committee in Milwaukee, discussed an Ohio utility company's study of one hundred randomly selected vehicular accidents for which they had full information. An analysis of those mishaps, in terms of the biorhythmic position of the person involved, indicated that sixty-eight percent of the accidents occurred on a critical day.

These are not by any means the only studies that have been done; they are, however, in many respects typical. Analysis occurs after the fact and in what could be called a one-to-one situation. The individual's birthday is used to compute his biorhythms for the day of an accident. If that day was a critical one, and if that person experienced a mishap on that day, then that finding validates, empirically at least, the biorhythm theory. And the percentages are fairly amazing. It is apparent that some sort of relationship between critical days and self-caused accidents does exist.

If in the case of the Ohio utility company, those sixty-eight persons had known they were experiencing critical days, would they still have had accidents? Most probably; but the number would more than likely have been smaller. Biorhythm theory does not claim to eliminate all mishaps, and should not be approached with that expectation. There is evidence, however, that biorhythms can, through an individual's awareness of his situation, significantly reduce the number of mishaps. As an example of the application of biorhythms in a safety program, consider the reports on Japanese firms, said to number in the thousands, that have made effective use of the theory.

Japanese Industrial Application of Biorhythm Theory

George Thommen, an advocate of biorhythms for more than twenty-five years, included in his book, *Is This Your Day?*, a letter from the Japan Biorhythm Association which describes the theory's enthusiastic adoption by industry—and a general reduction of thirty-five to forty percent in accident claims. One of the widely publicized examples is the Omi Railroad, which also operates hundreds of buses and taxis. The combination of advising drivers of their critical days, of rewarding them for such days completed without mishap, and of utilizing more traditional safety procedures has helped one of Omi's divisions to achieve over four million accident-free kilometers. During the first year that biorhythms were used in the safety program, the accident rate among Omi bus drivers reportedly fell fifty percent. Another Japanese firm, the Seibu Transport Company, assigned keypunch operators to different tasks on their critical days. The result? Mistakes were reduced by thirty-five percent.

Studies and reports such as these offer some empirical evidence for the influence of biorhythms on an individual's performance. They also raise certain legitimate questions. It has been suggested, for instance, that an employee should be given time off on his critical days, or that unions would object to their members being assigned other work. Mr. Anderson insists that since a critical day does *not* incapacitate an individual, alternative tasks should be considered only when the job is particularly hazardous. In most cases, reassignment on the six or so critical days per month is simply impractical. The more realistic and practicable approach seems to be to advise the employee of his critical days, so he can be alert to his own performance, and to notify his supervisor as well. Similarly, an executive could be made aware that his capabilities do fluctuate, thereby eliminating at least some of the anxiety that often accompanies those times when inability seems the order of the day.

Current Research

Another question arises in this brief outline of the methods often used to test biorhythms' viability. Certainly, those methods seem to partake of the Tuesday-morning-quarterback syndrome. And there is no attempt to deal with troublesome problems of the actual origination and the duration of the cycles. These considerations, among others, reveal the need for solidly scientific research into the theory itself and its possible uses in industry. And such work is in progress.

Dr. Douglas E. Neil, of the Naval Postgraduate School in Monterey, California, has been engaged in several projects to determine the relationship between biorhythms and the variance in human performance. Preliminary studies, involving analysis of accident claims, indicated that such a relationship does exist and is significant in terms of the low phase and the critical day. But using accident information limits the investigation: there is, effectively, only one sample point (the occurrence of the mishap) for each individual; so analysis does not treat the biorhythmic cycles as entities.

Dr. Neil designed an experiment in a controlled laboratory setting in which for seventy days subjects performed an information-processing task. Analysis revealed that of fourteen observed cycle changes, nine fell within one day of the critical times in one of the biorhythmic cycles. In Dr. Neil's words:

> Therefore, all subjects had significant periods within one day of 11.5, 14 and 16.5, critical points in the "Biorhythm" curves. The probability of this occurrence by chance is .015.

These studies are in his paper "Biorhythms and Industrial Safety" presented at the National Safety Congress (October 1974).

Dr. Neil is involved in other research projects into biorhythms. One is a 120-day study of the decision-making process, and he also plans an investigation into the relationship between biorhythms and productivity in industrial piecework. It is his view that biorhythms, an expression of the cyclical expenditure and conservation of an individual's energy, are one of the several factors in human performance. In that context, critical days can be put in proper perspective: such states of flux do exist but they are a challenge, they can be dealt with. Dr. Neil's work thus far suggests as well the importance of cyclical lows in terms of performance. Although the results of his studies and detailed discussions of his procedural techniques are not all available at this time, the directions in which he is working seem most promising and may lead to sensible implementation of biorhythms in industrial safety programs where they would be beneficial.

American Application of Biorhythm Theory

As a result of the interest in biorhythms generated by much of the above-mentioned research, and in spite of the controversy surrounding the theory, companies in the United States are seriously examining biorhythm's concepts and applicability. Cyrus B. Newcomb, Jr., was instrumental in devising a biorhythm-oriented safety program for that Ohio utility company. In 1973, United Air Lines' San Francisco Office of Industrial Engineering, working closely with Dr. Neil, initiated a program to explore the implications and possible applications of biorhythms. All United organizations received information about the theory and about general procedures—how employees would be made aware of their zero (or critical) days, how accidents would be recorded. If a particular facility asked to be included, supervisors there received a computer printout listing of zero days for a three-month period for their personnel and more specific instructions about procedure. At the end of that time, supervisors were to submit their subjective reactions to the use of biorhythms in a safety program and to indicate whether they had found a correlation between employees' zero days and accidents, and whether they desired materials for another ninety-day interval. Approximately

16,800 United employees in several departments at the maintenance bases in San Francisco and ten other cities have participated, some for only three months, others for longer periods of time. Most of the organizations which used the program during 1974 showed a reduction in the number of injuries. In addition, pilots, as a group, seem less susceptible to the influence of biorhythmic cycles than do the maintenance crews. A United spokesperson suggested that perhaps the reason was that the pilots' intensive screening and training make them more able to deal with and overcome the effects of a zero day.

Although follow-up studies were concluded in June, 1975, United has indicated that it does not intend to distribute either specifics of the program or its results. But people at United seem to feel that biorhythms can be useful as part of an overall accident-prevention program.

In spite of the exploratory nature of the project at United, some reports have made it seem that United, totally committed to the validity of biorhythms, rushed into the fray, scattering charts in its wake. That was and is not the case. But United's experience may be typical of the problems confronting many companies in the United States which are interested in finding out about and testing biorhythms, with an eye to possible integrating them into their safety programs. And United has been virtually inundated with requests for information from all over the world. Because study of biorhythms is not an established science, and because it is popularly (though mistakenly) consigned to the outer darkness of the occult, an organization that might examine the potential benefits seems to commit a gross breach of decorum. A more reasonable climate of opinion would allow unprejudiced investigation of this promising area. But the rumor mill continues to play fast and loose with that sort of corporate concern—yesterday it was Allegheny Air Lines, today the Los Angeles Rams, tomorrow the telephone company. It should not be surprising, then, that official denials or refusals to be named are frequent. But various organizations have been and are inquiring into biorhythms: Bernard Gittelson, of the Time Pattern Research Institute, states that his firm is involved in one- to two-year exploratory programs with fifty well-known companies.

Once the results become available, they will perhaps encourage other firms to investigate biorhythms. The figures so far indicate that they are indeed worthy of serious study. In the meantime, if you are an employer, and if you are thinking about using biorhythms in your company's accident-prevention program, you might try to respond to the following questions, devised by R. K. Anderson Associates to facilitate their consulting work.

1. How many employees are in your plant?
2. How many employees work at hazardous operations?
3. How closely is plant supervision maintained?
4. Who is directly responsible for supervision in each department?
5. How much are you willing to spend in time or labor costs to secure information about biorhythms?

6. Do you think it necessary to chart every employee?
7. Do you have someone in management who can devote the time to make the necessary studies?

Your answers can help you determine whether biorhythms can be of use to you. Time Pattern Research Institute is one of several companies which will provide employees' charts and information on how to use biorhythms in your particular situation. The procedure used by Time Pattern Research Institute is as follows: an industry is required to order at least one hundred charts and the charge is one dollar per name per year. A meeting is then held with personnel managers in that industry to inform them how to advise their employees about biorhythms. Usually, a test is devised wherein one hundred employees use biorhythms and another hundred are told nothing except "be careful." And, as Bernard Gittelson, Director of the Institute, points out, "Our results have shown that those who used biorhythm were better off, as accidents were reduced by as much as fifty percent."

If you are interested in one way of reducing the number of accidents in your firm, you might well consider biorhythms, which, when properly presented, can open a new channel of communication between employee and supervisor and create safety awareness on a more personal basis.

5 HOW TO DO YOUR OWN BIORHYTHM CHART

Figuring where you are, biorhythmically speaking, is not a difficult process. You merely find out how many complete cycles have already passed and how far advanced the next one is. Tables and an example are provided here to make the task even easier. But if a how-to chapter involving mathematics evokes fear and trembling in you, there are several firms whose computers will do the work for you. Be assured, however, whether or not you're experiencing an up day intellectually, the calculations will not take much time.

First, you total up the number of days lived. That sum is divided by the number of days in each cycle. Then you can plot your chart or anyone else's. The following example will show you how it's done.

Say you were born December 10, 1952; it is now June 5, 1973, and you want to determine the position of each biorhythmic cycle for that date. First you find the number of days that have passed since your birth, up to and including June 5, 1973. On your last birthday (December 10, 1972), you were twenty. Appendix 1 lists, for your convenience, each age and its equivalent in days. You'll see that twenty years equals 7,300 days. But you also have to add a day for each leap year. Appendix 2 makes this step a bit easier: count the number of *complete* leap years that have passed since your birth date, that is, how many February 29's you've lived through. In this case, the total is five. So from your day of birth up to and including your last birthday, you have lived 7,305 days.

Now, to get from December 10, 1972, to the day in question, June 5, 1973, begin by determining the number of days left in 1972. From the tenth of December to the thirty-first is twenty-one days. In Appendix 3 you'll find the number of days *between* January 1, 1973, and June 5, 1973. Be sure to add one day to include June 5. The total is 157 days. As of June 5, 1973, then, your age in days is the sum of these calculations or:

7305	days from December 10, 1952, to last birthday, including leap years
21	days from December 10 to December 31, 1972
157	days from January 1, 1973, up to and including June 5, 1973
7483	grand total or your age in days

While you rest on your laurels, consider the next step. All you do is divide that total by the number of days in each cycle. To find the position of your physical cycle on June 5, 1973, divide 7,483 by 23.

$$
\begin{array}{r}
325 \text{ completed physical cycles} \\
23\overline{)7483} \\
69 \\
\hline
58 \\
46 \\
\hline
123 \\
115 \\
\hline
8 \text{ days into a new cycle}
\end{array}
$$

For the sensitivity cycle on June 5, 1973, divide 7,483 by 28. The result is 267 completed cycles and 7 days into a new cycle.

For the intellectual cycle, dividing 7,483 by 33 equals 226 completed cycles, plus 25 days into a new one.

Preparing a Biorhythm Chart

After checking your calculations, you can prepare your biorhythm chart. You'll need a linear calendar with equal spaces allotted for each day and with a horizontal line drawn through the center. In Appendix 4 you will find a blank calendar and three templates (Appendix 5), one for each of the biorhythmic cycles. You can either cut them out or trace them and use the outlines as patterns for shaping cardboard or some other relatively stiff material. With the horizontal line of the linear calendar as a guide, place the eighth day on the template for the physical rhythm directly over June fifth and just draw in the outline of the curve. A similar procedure, using the sensitivity and intellectual templates, will give you their positions on the calendar.

Analyzing Your Chart

Your chart for June, 1973, (given your birth date of December 10, 1952) would look like this:

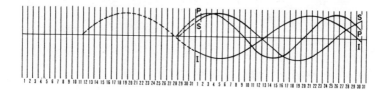

Fig. 27. Biorhythm chart for June 1973
(birth date Dec. 10, 1952)

And what does all that mean? The first critical day occurs in the physical cycle on June 9, when the sensitivity rhythm has passed its high point and when the intellectual rhythm is on an upswing. In general terms, that particular combination would indicate a transitional (critical) phase with the potential for mishap increased by the downward trend of the sensitivity cycle. That statement would, of course, be qualified by the effects of your personality and by your circumstances. There is *no* guarantee that you'll get sick or have an accident just because you experience a critical physical day. But the "maybe" inherent in this state of flux should be considered. On the ninth, you might take care not to become involved in strenuous activities, you might pay a bit more conscious attention when you drive.

But June 12 and 13 might not pass unnoticed: critical sensitivity and intellectual days fall within twenty-four hours of each other, and the physical rhythm is approaching a full low. Russell K. Anderson has found that when an accident does occur, and when the individual involved is in that biorhythmic position, the proximity to the median line of the crossing of two cycles can be an indication of the seriousness of the mishap. In this particular chart, you can see how close to the line the crossing of the sensitivity and intellectual cycles is. So these two days, the twelfth and the thirteenth, should probably not be treated like simply any other old day. The low physical rhythm means that you may tire rather easily, and that you're not likely to be in physical command. On the critical days, you might be edgy and inclined to grouse and your mind may be less than acute. But if you're aware of the potential on those two days, you can, in fact, go about your business and compensate by giving yourself extra time to consider details and by making an effort to think carefully about what you do. June 12 and 13 can be dealt with, but better to do it with your eyes open, instead of blindly rushing into and around the obstacles that may appear to spring up.

On the twentieth, there's another critical physical day, this time with the sensitivity cycle in low and the intellectual rhythm approaching a peak. This could be a just-feel-blue day or, depending on how you usually handle things, it might be a good one, with the intellectual high predominating. Again, the influence of all the biorhythmic situations depends on you, your circumstances and other factors, and on how you use your awareness of those situations.

Biorhythms are not in any sense predictive, they say nothing about future events. They do deal in probability; an individual experiencing a critical day is three to four times more accident-prone than at other times. Odds like that merit some attention. What kind of attention is really up to you. But there's something valuable and exciting in being able to know when you should be more aware of yourself and of your environment, and in being able to use that knowledge. Biorhythms offer you a way of keeping in tune with your own stores of energy and of expending or conserving them in positive ways.

6 THE COMPOSITE

A biorhythm chart represents the three cycles in as many lines, showing your highs, lows, and critical days. This graphic view of at least three of the patterns in your life does not take into account your personality or your situation. It's up to you to interpret the cyclical influences, to become aware of how you deal with them. That's what makes your biorhythm chart significant for you personally.

The composite, developed especially for this book, can be more directly relevant to you, for it takes into account, at least in general terms, how you see yourself. The composite is both a refinement and a further explanation of the biorhythm chart. In many cases, the single line can be a more precise demonstration of your particular cycles. You can of course do it yourself, with the aid of the examples that follow. The process does take time and does require some care. So if your very soul quailed before the calculations in the previous chapter, you should know that Human Bio Rhythms Corporation, mentioned earlier, will do it for you: you'll receive your biorhythm chart and interpretations, and your composite for a year.

How to Calculate Your Own Composite

Let's assume, once again, that your birth date is December 10, 1952; your biorhythm chart for June 1973 looked like this:

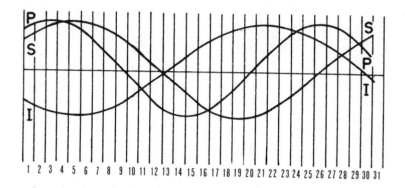

Fig. 28. Hypothetical chart for June 1973

The information contained in this chart can be represented in another manner, one which will lead to the determination of the composite.

First of all, on a sheet of paper—graph paper with quarter-inch squares is best—make a calendar for the month of June, with space enough for each day and for the vertical placement of the initials for each cycle and the composite (see Figure 29). The calendar can be done for any period of time, but for this example, use just the one month, June. Be sure to leave some space between each day.

Under each date, you're going to enter the appropriate day of each cycle, "I" for the intellectual, "S"

70

Day   1   2   3   4   5   6   7
I
S
P
C

Day   8   9   10   11   12   13   14
I
S
P
C

Day   15   16   17   18   19   20   21
I
S
P
C

Day   22   23   24   25   26   27   28
I
S
P
C

Day   29   30
I
S
P
C

Fig. 29. Linear calendar of composite
June 1973

for the sensitivity, and "P" for the physical. The "C" for composite will be entered last. In this case, the numbers we'll be using are those we found in the previous chapter. On June 5, 1973, the intellectual cycle was on the twenty-fifth day, the sensitivity rhythm was on the seventh day, and the physical cycle was on the eighth day. On the calendar you've constructed, enter "25" for the "I" cycle under June 5. Count back to the first, and then ahead to the thirtieth, filling in one "I" cycle day for each day of the month. For the "S" rhythm, enter "7" under June 5; the "P" cycle would be started with "8" under June 5. And both would be completed in the same manner as the "I" rhythm. Your calendar, with all biorhythm information added, should bear a resemblance to Figure 30.

Analyzing Your Personality Type

Now, set the calendar aside for a moment. In order to be able to fill in the spaces between each date with an assigned value for each cycle day, you need to determine what general type of person you are, biorhythmically speaking. The following nine questions are provided for that purpose. Your responses will be most valid if you answer quickly—don't spend too much time mulling over possible qualifying statements you'd like to make—and honestly. You can use a piece of scratch paper to record your answers (only one in each case).

1. In a minor crisis, do you: A. Remain calm and collected? B. Tend to weep? C. Attack the situation?
2. Do you prefer: A. To play games which challenge your thinking? B. To attend the

Day	1	2	3	4	5	6	7
I	21	22	23	24	25	26	27
S	3	4	5	6	7	8	9
P	4	5	6	7	8	9	10
C							

Day	8	9	10	11	12	13	14
I	28	29	30	31	32	33	1
S	10	11	12	13	14	15	16
P	11	12	13	14	15	16	17
C							

Day	15	16	17	18	19	20	21
I	2	3	4	5	6	7	8
S	17	18	19	20	21	22	23
P	18	19	20	21	22	23	1
C							

Day	22	23	24	25	26	27	28
I	9	10	11	12	13	14	15
S	24	25	26	27	28	1	2
P	2	3	4	5	6	7	8
C							

Day	29	30
I	16	17
S	3	4
P	9	10
C		

Fig. 30. Linear calendar with cycle days, June 1973

theater? C. To engage in active sports?
3. When you have to make a decision, do you: A. Carefully select the best option? B. Depend on intuition? C. Use trial and error?
4. Would someone who knows you well describe you as: A. Logical? B. Impulsive? C. Physically strong?
5. Are your life activities primarily: A. Analytic? B. Artistic? C. Psychomotor?
6. Would you characterize yourself as primarily: A. Intellectual? B. Emotional? C. Physical?
7. Would you, assuming you have the qualifications, prefer to be: A. A scientist? B. A performing artist? C. A professional athlete?
8. If you had to discipline a dependent child, would you: A. Select a punishment appropriate to the act committed? B. Become too sensitive and avoid the punishment? C. Give the child a spanking?
9. In your leisure time, do you prefer: A. To read? B. To watch television? C. To work with your hands?

Add up the number of A's, B's, and C's you selected. If there are five or more in any one category, you are considered that type: intellectual (the A's), emotional (the B's), or physical (the C's). Other combinations mean you are average with a tendency toward the category where most of your choices lie. "Average" should be used for someone you don't know well, or for cases in which the questionnaire is impractical.

Let's assume that you, still having the birth date of December 10, 1952, also answered those questions and, after adding your choices, you turned out to be average. Appendixes 6 through 9 (at the end of the book) show an assigned value for each day of each cycle, depending on category. Choose the table which is headed according to your self-classification as determined by your responses to the questionnaire. In this case, we'll use Appendix 6, average.

On that calendar for June, in the spaces you strategically left between each day, write in the appropriate value for each day of each cycle. Be sure to include the plus or minus sign. The completion of this step, with only the "C" spaces to be filled in, should produce the result found in Figure 31. Each of the values can then be used as a point on a graph, so you can plot each cycle. On graph paper (ten squares to the inch), consider each small square equal to .1 on the vertical axis, and two small squares equal to one day on the horizontal axis. The fruit of your labors is shown in Figure 32. This graph and the chart at the beginning of this chapter are different representations of the same situation: a biorhythm chart indicating highs, lows, and critical days. You can use either form, but the graph is the necessary preliminary for the composite.

To determine the composite for June 1973, return once again to your calendar. For each day, find the mathematical sum of the values assigned to the cycles and enter the totals in the spaces left for "C," the composite. For June 1, the sum of values (as shown in Figure 31) is +.6; for June 2, the total is +.9; and so on, for each day in the month. And the results are used to plot the single line. A full chart showing all three biorhythm cycles and the composite is found in Figure 33.

That single line, in effect, tells you a bit more about the configuration of your biorhythm chart.

Day	1		2		3		4		5		6		7	
I	21	−1.4	22	−1.7	23	−2.0	24	−2.3	25	−2.4	26	−2.1	27	−1.8
S	3	+1.2	4	+1.6	5	+2.0	6	+2.4	7	+2.8	8	+2.4	9	+2.0
P	4	+ .8	5	+1.0	6	+1.1	7	+ .9	8	+ .7	9	+ .5	10	+ .3
C		+ .6		+ .9		+1.1		+1.0		+1.1		+ .8		+ .5

Day	8		9		10		11		12		13		14	
I	28	−1.5	29	−1.2	30	− .9	31	− .6	32	− .3	33	0	1	+ .3
S	10	+1.6	11	+1.2	12	+ .8	13	+ .4	14	0	15	− .4	16	− .8
P	11	+ .1	12	− .1	13	− .3	14	− .5	15	− .7	16	− .9	17	−1.1
C		+ .2		− .1		− .4		− .7		−1.0		−1.3		−1.6

Day	15		16		17		18		19		20		21	
I	2	+ .6	3	+ .9	4	+1.2	5	+1.5	6	+1.8	7	+2.1	8	+2.4
S	17	−1.2	18	−1.6	19	−2.0	20	−2.4	21	−2.8	22	−2.4	23	−2.0
P	18	−1.0	19	− .8	20	− .6	21	− .4	22	− .2	23	0	1	+ .2
C		−1.6		−1.5		−1.4		−1.3		−1.2		− .3		+ .6

Day	22		23		24		25		26		27		28	
I	9	+2.2	10	+1.9	11	+1.6	12	+1.3	13	+1.0	14	+ .7	15	+ .4
S	24	−1.6	25	−1.2	26	− .8	27	− .4	28	0	1	+ .4	2	+ .8
P	2	+ .4	3	+ .6	4	+ .8	5	±1.0	6	+1.1	7	+ .9	8	+ .7
C		+1.0		+1.3		+1.6		+1.9		+2.1		+2.0		+1.9

Day	29		30	
I	16	+ .1	17	− .2
S	3	+1.2	4	+1.6
P	9	+ .5	10	+ .3
C		+1.8		+1.7

Fig. 31. Linear calendar with "average" assigned values

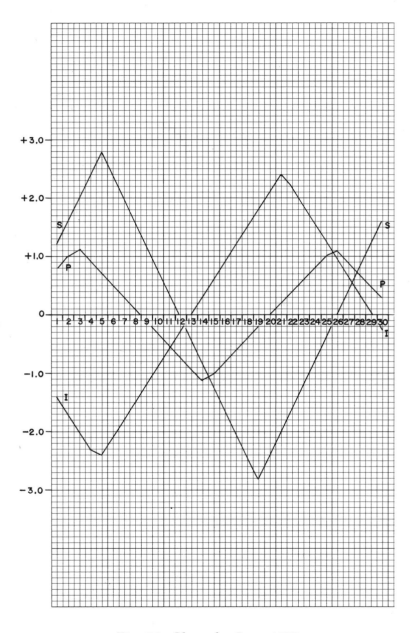

**Fig. 32. Chart for June 1973
(birth date Dec. 10, 1952), Average**

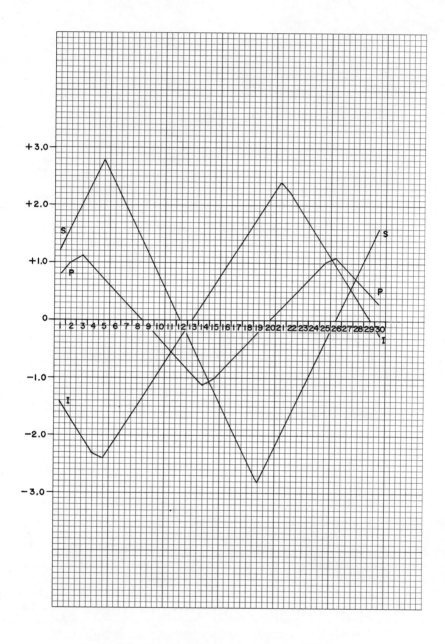

Fig. 33. Chart showing cycles and composite
June 1973, Average

The composite suggests the general flow of your energies during the course of this particular (and, again, hypothetical) month of June 1973. The critical days, on the ninth and twentieth, should be taken note of. But look at the situation on the twelfth and thirteenth. Critical sensitivity and intellectual days, falling within twenty-four hours of each other in the biorhythm chart, are represented in the composite as a continuing rush to a low. That does deserve some attention. It seems that special awareness is called for, to help compensate for what could be a more accident- or error-prone time than usual. The rise from that nadir, even with the slight tapering off at the end of the month, suggests increasing good feelings and physical ability, not to mention a probable improvement in mood.

An important word of caution, however. Although the composite acknowledges a general personality type and is, in that sense, perhaps a clearer reflection of how you see yourself than is the three-line biorhythm chart, that single line says nothing about future events. It is not a guarantee of mishap or of success. The composite, like the biorhythm chart, indicates potentials. And because it is a single line, it can be used more efficiently in compatibility studies, in which composites for two people are shown together. Potentials for a relationship, or dynamics that are worthy of note, can be spotted easily. But the interpretation takes a bit more time.

How Your Character Affects Your Composite

Through the course of this chapter, "average" has been the type used as an example. What difference does a change in category make? If you answered the

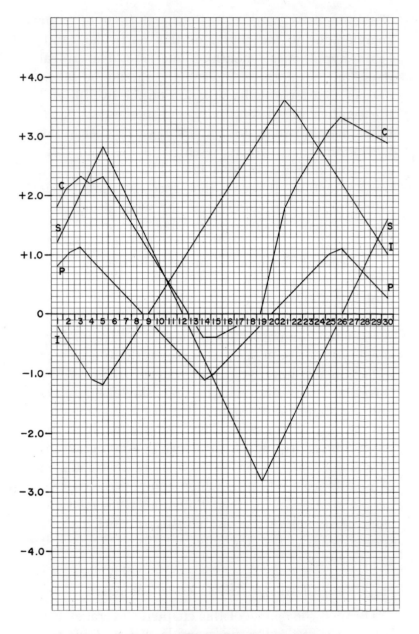

Fig. 34. Chart for June 1973
(birth date Dec. 10, 1952), Intellectual

questionnaire with five or more A's, you would be considered intellectual. If we use the perennial birth date of December 10, 1952, and examine the same month (June 1973), how would the cycles and the composite look? Using the procedure outlined above —setting up the calendar, entering under the June 5 date "25" for "I," "7" for "S," "8" for "P," and completing the cycles—you would then turn to Appendix 7, the intellectual type, to find the assigned values for each day of each cycle. And the sum of those figures would give you the means to plot the composite. Figure 34 presents the completed graph.

A comparison of the graphs in Figures 33 and 34 shows what the change from "average" to "intellectual" means: the intellectual cycle is augmented, as is the composite. And the critical intellectual day now occurs on the ninth, instead of on the thirteenth, and coincides with a critical physical day. An intellectual individual would be well advised, though, according to his composite, to pay particular attention to the thirteenth and the nineteenth. Those are the only two switch points during the month, compared to five in the three-line biorhythm chart itself. In many cases, composite crossings may prove more significant than the critical days. And perhaps the composite offers the most convincing argument against regarding those times of flux as fated bad days. What the single line shows you is the possibility of dealing positively with the challenge of critical days, particularly in terms of your own personality. The composite needs your awareness to be effective. It is not designed to supplant your biorhythm chart, but rather to enhance it, and to make your interpretation more relevant to you.

7 THE NATURE OF COMPATIBILITY

Being able to get along with someone doesn't necessarily mean that you and the other person must exemplify the peas-in-a-pod theory. The two of you can have, as they say, your differences. If the relationship is important to you, you probably make some sort of mutual allowances for disparities in, say, certain matters of taste. And compatibility often hinges on just that kind of compromise. Sometimes, though, you can get locked into viewing a relationship only one way: what becomes the balance of power can depend on manipulation for its familiar, perhaps painful, stability. In that situation, instead of being able to give, maybe you just get taken: the spirit of concession is lost.

Biorhythms can offer you a perspective on your personal relationships that may make identifying and dealing with a problem a bit easier. Biorhythm theory is a statement about cyclical changes, and their manifestation is largely a function of your temperament and of other external factors. But alterations in mood, in physical ability, and in brain power are experienced by everyone. Learning about those ups and downs in another person will not change them. But because the information is not gleaned from the actual situations, you may gain some insight into scenes whose meaning has been regularly escaping you.

Biorhythm Chart Comparisons

You can compare your biorhythm chart with someone else's covering the same time period. Perhaps the charts show similar patterns in sensitivity, totally different intellectual rhythms, and rather noncommittal physical cycles. If you two are of the same general personality type, the sensitivity coincidence could indicate one level of compatibility, because your emotional energies discharge and recharge at similar intervals. But if one of you is more excitable and the other more physically oriented, the result of close sensitivity cycle changes may be an antagonism not suggested by your actual charts. And the other two rhythms may perform compensatory functions. All in all, trying to examine the six cycles in two charts may prove confusing, and therefore hardly enlightening.

The Composite Perspective

The biorhythm composite simplifies the approach to a compatibility study. Once you perform the calculations described earlier, you have only two lines to consider. The composite has reference to certain general personality types, qualified by the individual's temperament and circumstances. But it's so easy to look at those lines, see wide differences, and leapingly conclude that the two people shouldn't even bother trying to spend time together. That's not necessarily true. The composite, like the biorhythm chart, shows changes in energy levels, not purely factual events. So "Be Aware" applies equally to similar composites and disparate ones, for neither is a guarantee of Eden or of the darker regions.

Biorhythmic Compatibility on the Job

The following chart is for the same one-month period for Barry and Nate, both physical types according to the questionnaire. They are assigned to work closely together in a plant. How will they get on during that month? One problem might occur toward the end of this period, when the difference between the composites is at its greatest. Barry's exuberance might irritate his partner, whose variation from low to high is smaller. But since they are both up, as it were, that potential might become good-natured banter. Minor differences of opinion could occur on the fifteenth and sixteenth. But if Barry and Nate were working on a project that had to be completed, they might not have a chance to begin to disagree. The composites crossing each other—on the second and the eleventh—indicate similar energy levels, but not similar reactions, because the lines are moving in opposite directions. The situations to be more aware of occur on five days: the second and the fifth for Barry, the third, twelfth, and twenty-second for Nate. Those times—

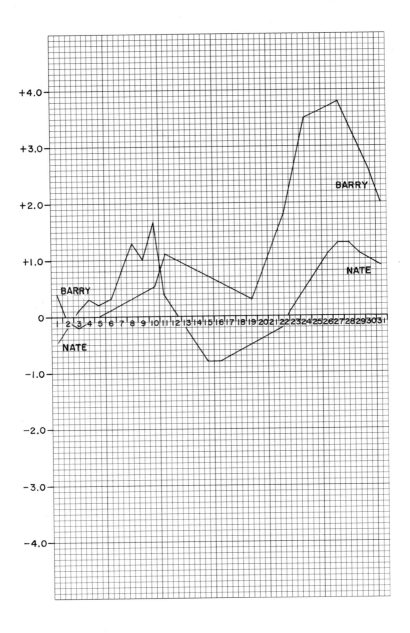

Fig. 35. Compatibility chart, Nate and Barry

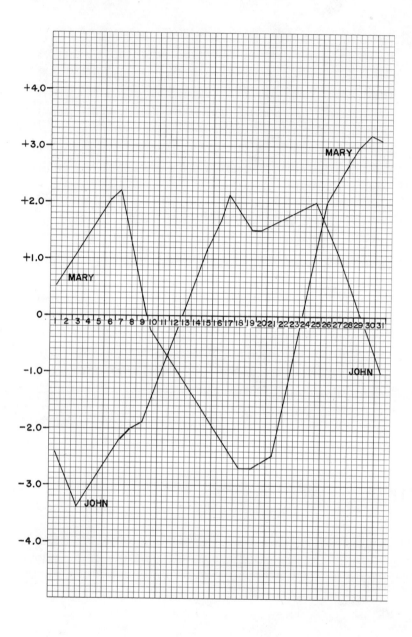

Fig. 36. Compatibility chart, Mary and John

the changes from plus to minus (or vice versa)—can be more significant in terms of potential for error than the critical days. These two men would be prudent to keep an unobtrusive eye on each other, particularly on the second and third, when each switch point is accompanied by a minus phase for the other. But on the basis of their chart (Figure 35), it would be fair to say that theirs is a good working relationship.

Charting a Marriage through Biorhythms

The next chart is for a married couple, both of whom are intellectual types. The variations in the composites are so wide, "compatibility" may seem the least relevant name for this chart. The only conjunctions occur on the eleventh and on the twenty-sixth, when the lines cross each other (one on the way up, the other on the way down). Not too promising! In terms of the cycle shifts—the ninth and twenty-fourth for Mary, the thirteenth and twenty-ninth for John—the changes occur at what seem to be inappropriate times, with little chance for mutual support. On the face of it, the chart appears to be a graphic representation of a deteriorating relationship, because the energy levels alter rather abruptly and in different rhythms. Perhaps the compromise needed is already part of the pattern of their relationship. They may be able to deal with the emotional situations in which they are at odds, and, generally, get along well.

But if that is not the case, if the divergences shown in the compatibility chart manifest themselves as continuing antagonisms and a backlog of resentment, perhaps just seeing the chart could be valuable. They would then have one way, a new way, of seeing their situation. The recognition of their differences could remove the pressure to change, to be better. And Mary and John might have a non-loaded way of talking about the way they behave.

The composite represents a personal configuration and is itself an indication that the influence of the biorhythmic cycles, once recognized, can be overcome. The chart is to be worked *with*, illuminated and informed by your own awareness. Although the basic circumstances won't be changed, perhaps you can gain a certain insight.

8 AND HOW TO COPE USING BIORHYTHMIC INFORMATION

Living *with* your life cycles, that's really the issue here. That means, first, knowing that cyclical fluctuations in physical, emotional, and intellectual energies, as shown in your biorhythm chart, do occur. Second, it means recognizing how those periodic changes in vitality affect you so you can get more in tune with your natural rhythms. When so many things seem to have gotten out of hand, beyond the individual's control, it only makes sense —and, perhaps, ensures sanity—to take charge wherever possible. And what better place to begin than with yourself?

After you do your biorhythm chart, or have it done, for a given period of time, you should consult it regularly. Some people look at their charts daily; others, occasionally, when they have to do something important; still others, only after an especially bad day. When you examine your chart for a given month, you should of course take note of the critical days, those times of transition when the body is shifting gears, and when there's an increased potential for error or accident. But you should also look at the highs and lows and consider which rhythms are involved. If those factors are then placed in the context of your own general personality type, you'll have a clear idea of what actions on which days may need extra attention.

If your chart shows, for example, a triple low on a day on which you have to be at your best to begin a new project at work, don't despair and immediately assume you'll blow the assignment. A more productive and positive response is to assess the situation in terms of your personality type, and then decide how best to compensate. If you are physically oriented, you'll be likely to tire more easily on that day, and so should take care not to overtax your body. If you are the emotional type, you could have a case of the blahs and should try not to sink into despondency. Or if you can be characterized as intellectual, you might feel as if your brain left town suddenly, and you should try to take time to stop and reflect in a situation which requires a decision. But no matter which personality type you are, you should take extra care when you drive and try to pay more attention to your surroundings. In that very awareness or alertness lies the way to overcome the effects of a triple low. If you know, you really can be prepared. Adjusting your expectations in this manner does not mean giving up. It does mean being kind to yourself, making reasonable demands on yourself, being attentive to your potentials, capabilities, and limitations. If that last smacks of failure, try to see it in the nonjudgmental framework offered by biorhythms.

Your chart is in effect a challenge. Awareness of some of the influences in your life can help you see that alterations previously thought of as a series of anthropomorphic zaps can be dealt with. They are, after all, *your* energies. A critical day signals a change, and if you're aware of that, you're no longer a victim. Say you have to drive a long distance on a critical sensitivity day. The trip should not be put off, no matter which general personality type you are. The positions of the other two rhythms could nullify the effects of this period of flux, especially a high in the physical or intellectual rhythm. But you should make every effort to stay alert, and if you find yourself falling into a highway-induced trance of mechanical action and reaction, you would be well advised to stop for a bit.

To use another example, you're giving a party to celebrate a young child's birthday; there will be fifteen other little boys and girls—and some of their mothers—and your chart shows a critical day in the physical and sensitivity cycles. You know you'll have to try for patience and for time so you don't get overly upset by the shenanigans that ice cream and cake seem to demand. But if you're aware of the internal tensions and their probable areas of expression, you'll be able to handle the party.

Highs, lows, and critical days are one way of formulating some of the variables in your life. It's up to you to determine how you act and react, how those cycles affect you. How to cope then becomes a question of *informed awareness,* a way of using biorhythms to get along with yourself. You can compensate when necessary, actively utilize your energies when appropriate. Accepting lows and highs is a means to self-tolerance and self-protection.

You can also gain an insight into the ups and downs of your relatives, friends, and business associates. If, for instance, you have an especially bad day at work because the boss finds fault with almost everything you say and do, a look at the boss's biorhythm chart could be revealing. It might show a double-critical day or a critical sensitivity day with the other two rhythms in low. If you know that, you might be a bit more tolerant both of the criticism and of yourself. And you won't have to take the day's upset home with you.

Or if a usually sympathetic friend seems snide and uncaring, his or her biorhythmic position could help you see one of the factors in an otherwise inexplicable personality change. You can then, perhaps, avoid making defensive and destructive statements to protect yourself from what seems to be an unwarranted attack.

But a word of caution: we aren't saying that knowing about biorhythm and actively using it in your life will make you all-forgiving, always smiling. We do believe that cyclical influences operate in all of us, and that it can be beneficial to have that awareness. You'll still have good days and bad days; you won't suddenly find yourself without the latter and the attendant errors or accidents. You will have a means of dealing with yourself and with others: biorhythms provide a positive way in which to view some of the fluctuations which are part of all our lives. More than that, they offer you a way of responding to the challenge, a way of taking charge, a way of taking care. And that is, after all, what coping is all about.

9 THE FUTURE OF BIORHYTHMS

The possible applications and uses of biorhythms extend into almost every area of human activity and endeavor. Since the theory is so promising, it should be studied and validated in a wide range of situations. Perhaps that time is coming, as evidenced by the work of Dr. Neil and many others, and by the number of companies involved in experimental programs based on the biorhythm theory.

Applications of Biorhythmic Theory

Planned Surgery

The theory of life's cadences can be used effectively in cases of planned surgery. A necessary but not emergency operation could be scheduled to coincide with the patient's own cycles of strength and of recuperation. This personalized scheduling would take into account mainly the patient's physical rhythm—which should ideally be approaching its peak—so the patient could best withstand the trauma of surgery. The patient also would have the further benefit of his own restorative and recuperative cycle when the physical rhythm switched into and proceeded through the low (or recharge) phase. Certainly, an operation performed when the patient was experiencing a critical physical day could allow chances for unnecessary complications. The patient's best chances not only for surviving the surgery but for a speedy recovery would be enhanced if the composite were used to determine the time of maximum physical, emotional, and intellectual stability. If biorhythms are used as a guide to the patient's general state of being, the operation itself will be more likely to be successful both immediately, in terms of correcting the problem, and later, in terms of the patient's recovery.

Several European hospitals routinely compute the patient's biorhythmic position in order to determine the scheduling for a surgical procedure that does not have to be completed on an emergency basis. Doctors have found that the period of incapacitation is thus significantly reduced, as is the duration of recovery. There are some surgeons, in fact, who will only operate when a patient's physical cycle is in the second to ninth day. The results of implementing biorhythmic theory in this way have been very good in Europe; perhaps American hospitals could explore this area—especially since there are such strong indications that it is in the patient's best interest.

It would be ideal, too, if the charts for all surgical staff involved could also be considered, so no one would be scheduled to participate if he or she were experiencing a critical day. In addition, the surgeon's awareness of his own biorhythmic position, as well as that of the patient, could only help create the most positive environment for the surgery. To be sure, surgeons must be able to overcome internal challenges, but knowing about biorhythmic influences might alert a surgeon to personal limitations at a given time. Increasing the odds in the patient's favor should be sufficient impetus to examine biorhythm theory in terms of this particular implementation.

Marriage Counseling

Biorhythms can have significant benefits in another area as well, marriage counseling. If a counselor has access to a couple's biorhythm and compatibility chart, he or she has a graphic insight into one aspect of their relationship, the ebb and flow of each person's energies and their respective states and receptivity when they come for counseling. Understanding, when fostered through the awareness biorhythms offer, can have a lasting effect, can change the course of a deteriorating relationship and remove the basic premise of confrontation. The charts can be another guide the counselor has at his or her disposal to demonstrate how some things change and that absolute consistency is neither desirable nor possible. In that context, it becomes clear that there's no need for hostile defensiveness, because at least one part of the relationship can be visualized and offers a common ground for meaningful communication. Simple awareness—often most difficult to sustain in a close relationship where taking-for-granted can easily replace appreciation—can produce dramatic results. Biorhythms are not a source; they can be a catalyst for that kind of awareness.

We have seen instances of precisely that development in some of our friends. Their quarrels had become epic battles, they were both miserable, and divorce became the primary topic of conversation. But having seen their composites, the regular changes in their energies as qualified by their general personality types, and how the composites look together, they had a way of dealing with their situation and with each other which left self and mutual destruction out of their particular equation. Having lessened the hostility and the pattern of hostile response, they then could deal with the human issues in their relationship more realistically, in a way which included the basic fact that each was subject to change.

A marriage counselor with biorhythm charts for the couple in question can contribute significantly by being able to point out what might be troublesome times—rhythms absolutely out of phase, for example, or rhythms (surprisingly enough) almost always in phase—and how discussions at these times might end in frustration, mutual recriminations. The counselor also has an indication of the couple's receptivity to new ideas, to being able to learn about themselves. Perhaps, too, the counseling period could be shortened, so the reliance of the couple on each other can be developed without an intermediary. Though the problems may still exist, the rhythms themselves have not changed. Day-to-day living can become easier with the recognition of sources of tension. Biorhythms should be examined as a possibility for becoming a working tool of the marriage counselor.

A Psychological and Psychiatric Aid

By extension, psychologists in other fields and psychiatrists could make use of their patient's biorhythm charts in counseling or therapy by being able to work more in concert with the patient's energies. A therapist could use biorhythms along with his or her professional expertise and knowledge of the patient to choose, for example, a time when the patient could best accept new ideas or when the patient could tolerate stress. Biorhythms could prove to be exceptionally valuable in these kinds of controlled situations.

There have been some preliminary indications that mental illness may operate cyclically. In the sixties, a project was initiated at Syracuse University to study the strength of electrical currents deep in the nerve stem of the brain and in the neuron cables in the spine, the arms and legs. Two schizophrenics and two normal patients were examined daily for two months. This so-called transcranial D.C. potential was observed to fluctuate in all four individuals, but a definitely cyclical pattern was also seen; the duration of the overall pattern was approximately twenty-eight days. The report of this experiment, published in the *New York State Journal of Medicine*, further stated that differences appeared between the patterns of the normal and the schizophrenic persons. Since the project was experimental, all findings need to be validated by further, intensive study, and although biorhythm theory was not used as a definition of the observed twenty-eight-day periodicity, research into cycles of certain types of mental illness could profitably use the theory, as one more empirical bit of data to be considered, another creative approach to the problem in general. Further research might indicate positive enough correlations between biorhythms and a schizophrenic's behavior, for example, to suggest that the theory could be implemented in treatment.

Special Education

The idea that the biorhythm chart and composite indicate propitious times for certain activities, whether emotional, physical, or intellectual, could be helpful also in teaching retarded children. A chart would show one aspect of the child's potential receptivity to new material and, therefore, the most beneficial and productive times for instruction. The chart would also show the times when consolidating material already learned would make the child feel less pressured. Perhaps in this way frustration and its frequent companion, rebellion, could be reduced, especially if the schedule coincided with the child's own personal timing. Biorhythms could be combined with knowledge of the child's behavior and personality to reflect more closely his internal pattern for learning. And then both the teaching and the learning processes could take place in a positive atmosphere.

Physical Therapy

Physical therapy could be scheduled to coincide with a child's physical highs. Recognizable gains could be made then; during the lows, other activities could be undertaken that wouldn't strain or frustrate the child, and he could proceed at his own rate. The applicability of a biorhythmically oriented program of physical therapy could be as beneficial for adults, when set up to take advantage of physical highs and to acknowledge the periodic recurrence of physical lows. The feasibility of incorporating biorhythms into such programs is a most fruitful area for research.

In all these instances—surgery, counseling, teaching, physical therapy, psychiatric care—biorhythms could be a major help to the people involved. We believe that study and research in those areas, among others, are necessary, so that the benefits of biorhythms can be made available as an accepted part of treatment. Anecdotal and empirical evidence suggests that it is an area certainly worth examining in detail.

Future Industrial Safety Programs

Another use of biorhythms is their applicability in programs of industrial safety and accident prevention. If employees and supervisors are aware of critical days, lows, and of the potential results of such days in the context of more traditional safety programs, studies thus far indicate that the number of accidents are reduced significantly. In this area, the Japanese have been pioneers. Companies in the United States—manufacturing, processing, and transportation—could certainly profit from following their example. If enough organizations not only experiment with biorhythmically oriented programs but are willing to publish their results, the theory would be well enough established to be an acceptable and accepted part of every safety program.

Perhaps then, as Bernard Gittelson has suggested, air line companies will advertise that "our pilots never fly on a critical day."

The possible uses of biorhythms in accident-prevention programs are being studied by a number of industries. The theory can be applied in other areas of industry as well. If, for instance, a company plans a large sales promotion seminar, it could be scheduled so that those in motivating roles would be at their most effective, experiencing only plus phases in intellectual and sensitivity rhythms particularly. Or if new research is to be undertaken, the timing of decision-making in designing the program could be such that the participants were at their best intellectually. The implications of this approach speak to a positive atmosphere for creativity, to real results for the company involved, and to unquestioned benefit for the people concerned because of reduced stress.

Biorhythms and Athletes

Athletes could use their biorhythm charts to help determine their training schedules. During the first eleven and a half days of the physical cycle, the discharge or plus phase, activities could be more strenuous, new exercises could be undertaken. During the second half of the cycle, a slower pace would be more in keeping with the need for rest and could include repetition of already learned exercises in sufficient quantity to preserve conditioning but not to strain. Athletes could in that way make fullest use of their energies and strengths while following the natural rise and fall of their capacities. There are, indeed, times to push yourself and times to rest. It makes sense to work in concert with those forces rather than at cross-purposes to them. Furthermore, attention to biorhythmic position before competition would allow an athlete to know how to direct his concentration, where extra effort might be needed to overcome difficulties in outlook, for example.

Golfers on the pro circuit have an extraordinarily hectic schedule, and they usually don't play in a few tournaments. Instead of randomly selecting those matches which they will not enter and playing when they are experiencing physical lows or critical days, they could use biorhythms as the basis for selecting the tournaments to play in. Often, failure for golfers, and for other athletes as well, can create a slump. One bad performance seems to get them down and to breed other poor performances. But if a golfer used his biorhythm chart to determine which matches he would not enter, according to his physical cycle, he could avoid the physical and emotional strain imposed by a slump.

Richard Phillips is currently doing research into the relationship between biorhythms and the individual baseball player's performance. He has done charts for all the Los Angeles Dodgers covering the entire 1975 season. When the Dodgers play, careful records are kept for each man on the team, with special attention given to the pitcher's performance. At the end of the season, all information will be coded and the computer printout will tell the story.

Conclusions

These are but a few examples of the ways in which biorhythms could be used beneficially. There are, to be sure, many questions about the theory which remain and which study and research should be undertaken to answer. For instance, what effects do the mother's rhythms have on her baby? How do the cycles operate at birth? Do they all go up, as is now theorized? Or do the rhythms descend? Do they, in fact, begin at the moment of birth? Or do they begin at the moment of conception? What relationship exists between biorhythms and the possibilities of determining a child's sex? What is the nature of the relationship between attitudes and biorhythms? Does failure, for example, increase one's vulnerability to lows? How do lows and critical days influence the time of death in older people? Is there a specific relationship between biorhythms and mental illness? What sort of connection is there between the cycles and accident-prone individuals?

Attempting to find answers to these questions will take time, effort, and money. But the extent of biorhythms' applicability and how they should be properly used would be among the conclusions of such research. It is clear to us that the theory deserves serious attention.

Biorhythm theory ultimately counsels self-knowledge; it is a way of understanding and a way of dealing with the changes we all experience. Additional study would allow people to accept the theory and be able to take advantage of it. People could become more aware of the need for rest—not artificial rest induced by alcohol or drugs—and could direct their energies positively. The potential offered by biorhythms for a greater sense of adjustment and well-being should not be ignored. As an aid, not as an end in itself, biorhythms can allow us to take charge of our lives and to take care of ourselves.

To have your biorhythm chart done by computer and interpreted by an expert, Richard V. Phillips, send your correct birth date and your name and address to:

Human Bio Rhythms Corporation
c/o Ward Ritchie Press
474 South Arroyo Parkway
Pasadena, California 91105

For $15, you'll receive your charts—showing the three cycles and the composite—covering a full year, plus interpretations.

BIBLIOGRAPHY

The initial works on biorhythms are in German and are, for the most part, extremely difficult to come by. This is not, therefore, a complete bibliography. The only works included are those that can be found in at least one library in the United States, whether the Library of Congress, the National Library of Medicine, or widely scattered university libraries.

More recent and more readily available works are also cited.

1. Origins of the biorhythm theory:

Fliess, Wilhelm. *Der Ablauf des Lebens: Grundlegung zur exakten Biologie* [The Course of Life: Foundation for an Exact Biology]. Leipzig and Vienna: Franz Deuticke, 1906.

―――. *Vom Leben und vom Tod* [Of Life and Death]. Jena: Eugen Diederichs, 1909.

————. *Zur Periodenlehre: Gesammelte Aufsätze* [On the Theory of Periodicity: Collected Lectures]. Jena: Eugen Diederichs, 1925.

Swoboda, Hermann. *Die Perioden des menschlichen Organismus in ihrer psychologischen und biologischen Bedeutung* [The Periodicity of the Human Organism in its Psychological and Biological Meaning]. Leipzig and Vienna: Franz Deuticke, 1904.

2. **Discussions and refinements of the theory:**

Früh, Hans R. *Rhythmenpraxis* [Practical Application of Rhythms]. Zurich: Verlag H. R. Früh, 1943.

————. *Triumph der Lebensrhythmen* [Triumph of the Rhythms of Life]. Büdingen-Gettenbach: Lebensweiser-Verlag, 1954.

Gross, Hugo Max. *Biorhythmik* [Biorhythmics]. Freiburg: Verlag Hermann Bauer, 1959.

————. *Hoch und Tief, unserer Lebensenergie* [High and Low, our Life Energy]. Aalen: Ebertin, 1953.

Riebold, Georg. *Einblicke in den periodischen Ablauf des Lebens* [Insights into the Periodic Course of Life]. Stuttgart: Marquardt, 1942.

Waldeck, Hans. *Ebbe und Flut im Menschen* [Ebb and Flood in Man]. Büdingen-Gettenbach: Lebensweiser-Verlag, 1952.

3. **Recent (and available) books about biorhythms:**

Thommen, George S. *Is This Your Day?* Rev. ed. New York: Crown Publishers, 1973.

Wernli, Hans J. *Biorhythm: A Scientific Exploration into the Life Cycles of the Individual.* Translated by Rosemary Colmers with the technical supervision of George Thommen. New York: Crown Publishers, 1960.

4. **Recent papers and articles:**

Anderson, Russell K. "Biorhythm—Man's Timing Mechanism," *American Society of Safety Engineers Journal*, February 1972, pp. 17-21.

Brady, Tim. "Bio What?" *TAC Attack*, March 1972, pp. 16-19.

Dreiske, Paul. "Strange Forces in Our Times." *Family Safety*, Summer 1972, p. 15.

Mackenzie, Jean. "How Bio Rhythms Affect Your Life." *Science Digest*, August 1973, pp. 18-22.

Neil, Douglas E. "Biorhythms and Industrial Safety." Summary of a paper read at the National Safety Congress, October 1974.

Newcomb, Cyrus B., Jr. "Bio-Rhythm Chart Report." Paper presented to the Edison Electric Institute Accident Prevention Committee, October 1974.

Shah, Diane K. "Biorhythms Blues." *The National Observer*, 7 December 1974.

Zito, Tom. "Pilots' Biorhythm Cycles Are Studied as Factors in Crashes." *The Washington Post*, 2 February 1975.

APPENDIX 1

Days Lived for Specific Ages

YEARS	DAYS	YEARS	DAYS	YEARS	DAYS	YEARS	DAYS
1	365	26	9490	51	18615	76	27740
2	730	27	9855	52	18990	77	28105
3	1095	28	10220	53	19340	78	28470
4	1460	29	10585	54	19710	79	28835
5	1825	30	10950	55	20075	80	29200
6	2190	31	11315	56	20440	81	29565
7	2550	32	11680	57	20805	82	29930
8	2920	33	12045	58	21175	83	30295
9	3285	34	12410	59	21535	84	30660
10	3650	35	12775	60	21900	85	31025
11	4015	36	13140	61	22265	86	31390
12	4380	37	13505	62	22630	87	31755
13	4745	38	13878	63	22995	88	32120
14	5110	39	14235	64	23360	89	32485
15	5475	40	14600	65	23725	90	32850
16	5840	41	14965	66	24090	91	33215
17	6205	42	15330	67	24455	92	33580
18	6570	43	15695	68	24820	93	33945
19	6935	44	16060	69	25185	94	34310
20	7300	45	16425	70	25550	95	34675
21	7665	46	16790	71	25915	96	35040
22	8030	47	17155	72	26280	97	35405
23	8395	48	17520	73	26645	98	35770
24	8760	49	17885	74	27010	99	36135
25	9125	50	18250	75	27375	100	36500

APPENDIX 2

Leap Years

1876	1928	1976
1880	1932	1980
1884	1936	1984
1888	1940	1988
1892	1944	1992
1896	1948	1996
1904	1952	2000
1908	1956	2004
1912	1960	2008
1916	1964	2012
1920	1968	2016
1924	1972	2020

APPENDIX 3

Computation of Days

JAN.	FEB.	MAR.	APR.	MAY	JUNE
1 - 1	1 - 32	1 - 60	1 - 91	1 - 121	1 - 152
2 - 2	2 - 33	2 - 61	2 - 92	2 - 122	2 - 153
3 - 3	3 - 34	3 - 62	3 - 93	3 - 123	3 - 154
4 - 4	4 - 35	4 - 63	4 - 94	4 - 124	4 - 155
5 - 5	5 - 36	5 - 64	5 - 95	5 - 125	5 - 156
6 - 6	6 - 37	6 - 65	6 - 96	6 - 126	6 - 157
7 - 7	7 - 38	7 - 66	7 - 97	7 - 127	7 - 158
8 - 8	8 - 39	8 - 67	8 - 98	8 - 128	8 - 159
9 - 9	9 - 40	9 - 68	9 - 99	9 - 129	9 - 160
10 - 10	10 - 41	10 - 69	10 - 100	10 - 130	10 - 161
11 - 11	11 - 42	11 - 70	11 - 101	11 - 131	11 - 162
12 - 12	12 - 43	12 - 71	12 - 102	12 - 132	12 - 163
13 - 13	13 - 44	13 - 72	13 - 103	13 - 133	13 - 164
14 - 14	14 - 45	14 - 73	14 - 104	14 - 134	14 - 165
15 - 15	15 - 46	15 - 74	15 - 105	15 - 135	15 - 166
16 - 16	16 - 47	16 - 75	16 - 106	16 - 136	16 - 167
17 - 17	17 - 48	17 - 76	17 - 107	17 - 137	17 - 168
18 - 18	18 - 49	18 - 77	18 - 108	18 - 138	18 - 169
19 - 19	19 - 50	19 - 78	19 - 109	19 - 139	19 - 170
20 - 20	20 - 51	20 - 79	20 - 110	20 - 140	20 - 171
21 - 21	21 - 52	21 - 80	21 - 111	21 - 141	21 - 172
22 - 22	22 - 53	22 - 81	22 - 112	22 - 142	22 - 173
23 - 23	23 - 54	23 - 82	23 - 113	23 - 143	23 - 174
24 - 24	24 - 55	24 - 83	24 - 114	24 - 144	24 - 175
25 - 25	25 - 56	25 - 84	25 - 115	25 - 145	25 - 176
26 - 26	26 - 57	26 - 85	26 - 116	26 - 146	26 - 177
27 - 27	27 - 58	27 - 86	27 - 117	27 - 147	27 - 178
28 - 28	28 - 59	28 - 87	28 - 118	28 - 148	28 - 179
29 - 29		29 - 88	29 - 119	29 - 149	29 - 180
30 - 30		30 - 89	30 - 120	30 - 150	30 - 181
31 - 31		31 - 90		31 - 151	

JULY	AUG.	SEPT.	OCT.	NOV.	DEC.
1 - 182	1 - 213	1 - 244	1 - 274	1 - 305	1 - 335
2 - 183	2 - 214	2 - 245	2 - 275	2 - 306	2 - 336
3 - 184	3 - 215	3 - 246	3 - 276	3 - 307	3 - 337
4 - 185	4 - 216	4 - 247	4 - 277	4 - 308	4 - 338
5 - 186	5 - 217	5 - 248	5 - 278	5 - 309	5 - 339
6 - 187	6 - 218	6 - 249	6 - 279	6 - 310	6 - 340
7 - 188	7 - 219	7 - 250	7 - 280	7 - 311	7 - 341
8 - 189	8 - 220	8 - 251	8 - 281	8 - 312	8 - 342
9 - 190	9 - 221	9 - 252	9 - 282	9 - 313	9 - 343
10 - 191	10 - 222	10 - 253	10 - 283	10 - 314	10 - 344
11 - 192	11 - 223	11 - 254	11 - 284	11 - 315	11 - 345
12 - 193	12 - 224	12 - 255	12 - 285	12 - 316	12 - 346
13 - 194	13 - 225	13 - 256	13 - 286	13 - 317	13 - 347
14 - 195	14 - 226	14 - 257	14 - 287	14 - 318	14 - 348
15 - 196	15 - 227	15 - 258	15 - 288	15 - 319	15 - 349
16 - 197	16 - 228	16 - 259	16 - 289	16 - 320	16 - 350
17 - 198	17 - 229	17 - 260	17 - 290	17 - 321	17 - 351
18 - 199	18 - 230	18 - 261	18 - 291	18 - 322	18 - 352
19 - 200	19 - 231	19 - 262	19 - 292	19 - 323	19 - 353
20 - 201	20 - 232	20 - 263	20 - 293	20 - 324	20 - 354
21 - 202	21 - 233	21 - 264	21 - 294	21 - 325	21 - 355
22 - 203	22 - 234	22 - 265	22 - 295	22 - 326	22 - 356
23 - 204	23 - 235	23 - 266	23 - 296	23 - 327	23 - 357
24 - 205	24 - 236	24 - 267	24 - 297	24 - 328	24 - 358
25 - 206	25 - 237	25 - 268	25 - 298	25 - 329	25 - 359
26 - 207	26 - 238	26 - 269	26 - 299	26 - 330	26 - 360
27 - 208	27 - 239	27 - 270	27 - 300	27 - 331	27 - 361
28 - 209	28 - 240	28 - 271	28 - 301	28 - 332	28 - 362
29 - 210	29 - 241	29 - 272	29 - 302	29 - 333	29 - 363
30 - 211	30 - 242	30 - 273	30 - 303	30 - 334	30 - 364
31 - 212	31 - 243		31 - 304		31 - 365

APPENDIX 4

Blank Calendar

		31
		30
		29
		28
		27
		26
		25
		24
		23
		22
		21
		20
		19
		18
		17
		16
		15
		14
		13
		12
		11
		10
		9
		8
		7
		6
		5
		4
		3
		2
		1

APPENDIX 5

Templates

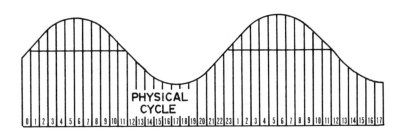

PHYSICAL CYCLE

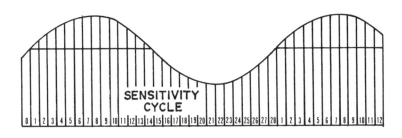

SENSITIVITY CYCLE

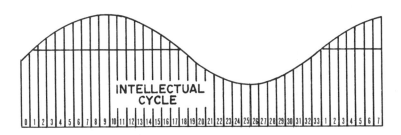

INTELLECTUAL CYCLE

APPENDIX 6

Average Personality Types

DAYS	I	S	P
1	+ .3	+ .4	+ .2
2	+ .6	+ .8	+ .4
3	+ .9	+1.2	+ .6
4	+1.2	+1.6	+ .8
5	+1.5	+2.0	+1.0
6	+1.8	+2.4	+1.1
7	+2.1	+2.8	+ .9
8	+2.4	+2.4	+ .7
9	+2.2	+2.0	+ .5
10	+1.9	+1.6	+ .3
11	+1.6	+1.2	+ .1
12	+1.3	+ .8	− .1
13	+1.0	+ .4	− .3
14	+ .7	0	− .5
15	+ .4	− .4	− .7
16	+ .1	− .8	− .9
17	− .2	−1.2	−1.1
18	− .5	−1.6	−1.0
19	− .8	−2.0	− .8
20	−1.1	−2.4	− .6
21	−1.4	−2.8	− .4
22	−1.7	−2.4	− .2
23	−2.0	−2.0	0
24	−2.3	−1.6	
25	−2.4	−1.2	
26	−2.1	− .8	
27	−1.8	− .4	
28	−1.5	0	
29	−1.2		
30	− .9		
31	− .6		
32	− .3		
33	0		

APPENDIX 7

Intellectual Personality Types

DAYS	I	S	P
1	+1.5	+ .4	+ .2
2	+1.8	+ .8	+ .4
3	+2.1	+1.2	+ .6
4	+2.4	+1.6	+ .8
5	+2.7	+2.0	+1.0
6	+3.0	+2.4	+1.1
7	+3.3	+2.8	+ .9
8	+3.6	+2.4	+ .7
9	+3.4	+2.0	+ .5
10	+3.1	+1.6	+ .3
11	+2.8	+1.2	+ .1
12	+2.5	+ .8	− .1
13	+2.2	+ .4	− .3
14	+1.9	0	− .5
15	+1.6	− .4	− .7
16	+1.3	− .8	− .9
17	+1.0	−1.2	−1.1
18	+ .7	−1.6	−1.0
19	+ .4	−2.0	− .8
20	+ .1	−2.4	− .6
21	− .2	−2.8	− .4
22	− .5	−2.4	− .2
23	− .8	−2.0	0
24	−1.1	−1.6	
25	−1.2	−1.2	
26	− .9	− .8	
27	− .6	− .4	
28	− .3	0	
29	0		
30	+ .3		
31	+ .6		
32	+ .9		
33	+1.2		

APPENDIX 8

Emotional Personality Types

DAYS	I	S	P
1	+ .3	+1.4	+ .2
2	+ .6	+1.8	+ .4
3	+ .9	+2.2	+ .6
4	+1.2	+2.6	+ .8
5	+1.5	+3.0	+1.0
6	+1.8	+3.4	+1.1
7	+2.1	+3.8	+ .9
8	+2.4	+3.4	+ .7
9	+2.2	+3.0	+ .5
10	+1.9	+2.6	+ .3
11	+1.6	+2.2	+ .1
12	+1.3	+1.8	− .1
13	+1.0	+1.4	− .3
14	+ .7	+1.0	− .5
15	+ .4	+ .6	− .7
16	+ .1	+ .2	− .9
17	− .2	− .2	−1.1
18	− .5	− .6	−1.0
19	− .8	−1.0	− .8
20	−1.1	−1.4	− .6
21	−1.4	−1.8	− .4
22	−1.7	−1.4	− .2
23	−2.0	−1.0	0
24	−2.3	− .6	
25	−2.4	− .2	
26	−2.1	+ .3	
27	−1.8	+ .6	
28	−1.5	+1.0	
29	−1.2		
30	− .9		
31	− .6		
32	− .3		
33	0		

APPENDIX 9

Physical Personality Types

DAYS	I	S	P
1	+ .3	+ .4	+1.0
2	+ .6	+ .8	+1.2
3	+ .9	+1.2	+1.4
4	+1.2	+1.6	+1.6
5	+1.5	+2.0	+1.8
6	+1.8	+2.4	+1.9
7	+2.1	+2.8	+1.7
8	+2.4	+2.4	+1.5
9	+2.2	+2.0	+1.3
10	+1.9	+1.6	+1.1
11	+1.6	+1.2	+ .9
12	+1.3	+ .8	+ .7
13	+1.0	+ .4	+ .5
14	+ .7	0	+ .3
15	+ .4	− .4	+ .1
16	+ .1	− .8	− .1
17	− .2	−1.2	− .3
18	− .5	−1.6	− .2
19	− .8	−2.0	0
20	−1.1	−2.4	+ .2
21	−1.4	−2.8	+ .4
22	−1.7	−2.4	+ .6
23	−2.0	−2.0	+ .8
24	−2.3	−1.6	
25	−2.4	−1.2	
26	−2.1	− .8	
27	−1.8	− .4	
28	−1.5	0	
29	−1.2		
30	− .9		
31	− .6		
32	− .3		
33	0		

INDEX

Page numbers for illustrations are in italics